CLAUDIA ZANLUNGO
DANIELA TARABRA

The Story of
BAROQUE ARCHITECTURE

PRESTEL
Munich · London · New York

CONTENTS

INTRODUCTION

During the 17th century Europe witnessed scenes of terrific contrasts. The horrific Thirty Years' War was raging (1618–1648) and the populace was besieged by fighting and religious conflict. Those who held the reigns of power devoted vast amounts of energy and resources to the display of their authority; whether royal or papal. Art and architecture were seen as the most effective means to display the *mise en scène* of presumed superiority and the illusory, propagandist representation of a vibrant and magnificent era that encompassed the Baroque period.

The period also witnessed Galileo and Copernicus' astonishing scientific discoveries, which signalled the end of anthropocentrism and revealed to what extent Renaissance values and theories had been vain and illusory. Artistic endeavours aimed to convert illusions into a plausible reality, blurring the lines between truth and lies. While Giambattista Marino, a famous Baroque poet, was proclaiming, "Marvel is the aim of the poet," artists and architects were experimenting with scenography and kowtowing to the élite using skills borrowed from the theatre to create a sense of melodrama. Designers also drew upon the radical new scientific discoveries at that time — especially in the field of optics — in order to trigger awe and wonder and to involve the spectator directly in the play of ambiguities created by figurative elements, light and space.

The aim of the artist was to provide the onlooker with an illusion of a world free of daily cares; though the works mostly did contain loaded references to the transience of life (as seen in many still life paintings of the period which featured the motto '*memento mori*' translated, 'remember you must die'). Artists also sought to communicate the truth of faith, the power of Rome and the corresponding absolute power '*di turno*' or torsion. Baroque architecture stood out prominently as being a wonderfully innovative fusion of science and art to create a harmonious blend of grandiose rhetoric and rational clarity.

Alongside the obvious formal elements — in stark contrast from those that had previously formed the basis for European architecture until after the Renaissance – Baroque picked up and expanded further on some of the late 16th century Mannerist stylistic trends. The taut curved lines, altered proportions and Classical harmony evident in some of Michelangelo's work (the gigantic dome of St Peter's, for example) triggered powerful reactions among his contemporaries and laid the foundation for the revolutionary aesthetic change that was to find its greatest expression in Rome between 1630 and 1670. Michelangelo was later to be recognised as the father of Baroque architecture.

Unlike the Mannerists, Baroque architects in Rome aspired to a powerful transformation of space, altering traditional architectural plans and elevations and not

Gian Lorenzo Bernini, *Ecstasy of St Theresa*, Cappella Cornaro, Santa Maria della Vittoria, 1647–1651, Rome Bernini (1598–1680) was the undisputed master of Baroque, as exemplified by this polychrome marble aedicule, where he managed to capture the exact moment at which the angel strikes St Theresa, petrifying the moment of passage between her earthly life and her ascent into heaven. The drama of the event is emphasised by the lighting effects produced by both direct and indirect light. The scene is top lit from a hidden window from which gilded stucco rays emanate, providing the background to the scene. The entire work has been treated as a veritable *mise en scène*. There is no perceptible boundary between the drama and the congregation, thus the onlooker is wholly drawn into the piece as a witness to this realistically depicted religious event.

confining themselves to decorative experimentation alone. Ironically Baroque was, and is even now, regarded as being purely decorative and superficial.

Despite the bitter criticism levelled at these architects for their disregard for traditional architecture, most of them were in actual fact extremely well-versed in Classical Roman architecture and drew extensively from their knowledge of Classical tenants in their Baroque work.

The majestic façades and forms drawn from the Antique were no longer simply being imitated, they were also being reinterpreted. It is also clearly evident that 17th century works borrowed extensively from Renaissance architecture and the Italianate style, especially from works by Andrea Palladio, Giacomo da Vignola and Sebastiano Serlio. Rome was the undisputed artistic hub of Italy as well as of Europe right up until the early 18th century. Thereafter, Baroque architecture began to spread northwards and southwards in Italy, where different variations were developed. In Piedmont, Guarino Guarini's (1624–1683) original style failed to take hold and Late Baroque was to take a different, but nevertheless unique, direction with the work of the Baroque architect, Filippo Juvarra.

Italy's independent states all developed their own particular versions of Baroque, although circumscribed by, sometimes ingenuous, regional expressions.

The spatial revolution sparked by Guarino Guarini and Francesco Borromini however, burgeoned in Europe, especially in Austria and Bohemia, where it became an important source of inspiration for the German Late Baroque. The new style established itself far more quickly than previous 17th century trends. This could be attributed to advances in travel, the parallel spread of Catholicism as well as the

Claude Perrault, east façade of the Louvre, 1667–1674, Paris
Perrault shows in this palatial project that he understands the new Roman trends: the plinth of the colonnade is traditionally Italian and the enormous columns (giant order) are Baroque in style. These elements have however, been treated with a strictly French approach: the aesthetic principles of 17th century French Baroque, as can be seen by the rigour of the straight lines of the façade that were based on Classicism. The façade may be exceedingly elongated, but it is far from monotonous: the complex relationship of the paired Classical columns with the background stonework plane of the façade creates an interesting rhythm.

publication of various architectural treatises. An illustrated, text-free version of Guarini's *Civil Architecture*, for example, was published in Bohemia in 1686. By the late 17th century, Paris had overtaken Rome as the European centre of the Baroque movement.

Spatial Forms

The earliest identifiably Baroque forms show the attempt to instil a more dynamic relationship between palaces – or churches – and the urban environment in which they were situated. Straight lines became curved, almost as if trying to extend internal spaces beyond the building envelope. The stone façades however, had to mark a division, acting as interfaces between inside and outside, which explains why the elevations were shaped and contorted into curves, as if to reduce and diminish the external confines of the building envelope. The undulating movement implied, derives from a series of tensions created by the conversion of dynamic, thrusting forces: the internal space seemingly expanding towards the exterior space while the street advances to meet it. In Late Baroque, the contrasting juxtaposition of concave and convex lines served to emphasise this tension — employed to create a sense of dynamic. The undulating and curvilinear movement of the lines gives the impression of infinite extension, while the effect of the expansion and contraction of the forms give the impression of a living, breathing organism. In the most sumptuous and accomplished works, such as those by Borromini and Guarini, this vital play of movement is a complex mechanism that works both in plan and in elevation: the lines and primary spatial elements are repeated, converge and are blended, thus providing an incredible sensation of dynamic continuity which, despite the complex geometry, can easily be perceived on a sensory level.

'The total work of art'

Unlike during the Renaissance era, when the individual artistic disciplines maintained their autonomy and were integrated organically within buildings, Baroque focused on the collaboration and unity of all the various artistic disciplines. As was the case with the earlier Gothic architecture, the 17th century principle stated that the individual arts should not remain segregated as they were deemded to lack the autonomy to achieve completion on their own.

Art was no longer a representation of the order of nature, as in the Humanist era, but artifice that orchestrated the *mise en scène* of an altered reality: sculpture and architecture sought a pictorial effect, while painting, with its perspectival play of optical illusion, became architectural and sculptural. Thus, the various artistic genres, both literary and pictorial, were forced into the service of the art of rhetoric, where artistic endeavour portrayed hyper-realistic images and scenes: space, light and figurative elements were all harnessed to this end. The architect, Gian Lorenzo Bernini, believed that unity could be created by the harmony of oppositions and therefore that the arts should be brought together to achieve sumptuous scenographies. These spaces would inspire the souls of the faithful and transform them into active spectators, thus instilling loyalty to the Roman Catholic Church and encouraging Faith itself.

Most 17th century architects had been trained as painters, sculptors or stonemasons, turning only later to the discipline of architecture. The practical skills they gathered helped them to complete the works of art they set out to achieve. Baroque artists were convinced by the expressive potential of ornamentation; in architecture Baroque was used to excess, unreservedly applied to every available surface in order to amaze and confuse the observer. The artists were entirely unscrupulous when it came the use of materials, which they used in every way possible in order to achieve the desired effect. The various component elements were primarily designed to create illusionary effects; thus marble, stucco, gold and copper were all given equal value. The

**Francesco Borromini,
San Carlo alle Quattro Fontane,
1638–1677, Rome**
This was the first time that a façade had been able to achieve such a high level of dynamism and spatial depth. Previously, conveying movement on façades had been achieved by adding undulating layers to surfaces: in this case however, movement appears to come from within the upper layer itself, as if animated by a vital force. The modification in the curve from the top to the bottom level is organically achieved and has no evident discontinuity (note the concave-convex-concave rhythm of the lower storey, demarcated by the stringcourse, whereas the upper storey has the rhythm concave-concave-concave). The oscillating rhythm is accompanied by the relief of the pendentives, culminating in the oval medallion which crowns the building.

boundary between function and appearance became even more blurred than before, as stucco, angels and other sculptural figures were also used to mask structural joins and to draw the eye of the observer away from any necessary architectural 'trickery'. Baroque architecture was rather like Gothic architecture in terms of its stance on decoration — the antithesis of Renaissance principles. In Baroque architecture, structure followed its own logic, while the superficial application of embellishments provided the aesthetic dimension. Renaissance architects, on the other hand, had used the various architectural orders as design tools, while also using them as decoration. Balanced proportions and overall harmony were deployed in the pursuit of beauty and truth. Baroque stuccoes and plastic elements were not designed to interact with the structure or function of the building, though played an important part in achieving the dramatic effect.

During the 18th century this passion for superficial decoration led to 'ornamentation for ornamentation's sake' in southern Germany, Spain, the Iberian colonies, as well as in southern Italy.

The significant role that light played in Baroque art was true of its role in Baroque architecture too. Light was manipulated for its ability to play on emotions and to rouse wonder and amazement in the onlooker. The pictorial luminosity of the 16th century was thus further explored and exploited during the 17th century. Paintings were characterised by the use of sombre, nocturnal effects and light sources such as candles and torches. The Italian master, Caravaggio, manipulated light to unique effect in his highly emotive paintings. Equally, architects working during the same period used both direct and natural light, as well as indirect or artificial light that was carefully manipulated in order to create theatrical atmospheres. Works by leading 17th century Italian Baroque architects are testament to their different approaches to light. Unlike Bernini, Borromini did not orchestrate invisible light sources, preferring rather to rely on the architectural forms themselves to obtain the desired visual and illusory effects. Borromini's use of light was far more architectural, but was by no means less creative or evocative than Bernini's.

opposite page
Gian Lorenzo Bernini, canopy over the main altar, 1624–1633, St Peter's Church, The Vatican
This gigantic bronze structure (almost thirty metres high) is the ultimate example of Bernini's talent for combining architecture and sculpture, making them seem to merge seamlessly. The canopy is situated on axis beneath Michelangelo's dome, restoring its original role of absolute dominion over the space, subsiding gradually as the nave continues. In this instance, the canopy serves to compliment the architectural space, interacting with it through the dynamic twisting movement created by the four tortile columns on which it rests. The vertical supports create a kind of dialogue with similar columns that flank the niches beneath the dome.

Michael Thumb, Christian Beer and Franz Beer, view towards the choir of the church of St Peter and Paul 1686–1692, Obermarchtal, Germany
The pure volumes of the space – articulated by powerful, austere piers – are covered and richly embellished with sumptuous stuccoes featuring plant motifs. The interior is painted entirely white, apart from the splashes of colour provided by the furnishings and the gold and silver of the altars.

In their capacity as hidden light sources, Guarini's punctured cupolas illustrated just how light could be juxtaposed with architectural surfaces, filtering through perforated structures, reflecting and refracting onto dark surfaces. The 17th century was the era during which science triumphed; the principles of Newtonian optics had an important role to play in the new scientific discoveries.

Architecture and Illusion

The Baroque era was marked by the enormous popularity of the great frescoes on the ceilings of churches and palaces. One particularly successful 17th century genre was *quadratura*, trompe l'œil views composed in painted architectural frames. This trend for trompe l'œil had become popular during the late Cinquecento and became extremely widespread in Italy and the rest of Europe during the 17th century. The dissemination could also be ascribed to the codification of perspectival rules in handbooks, especially after the publication in 1693 of *Perspectiva Pictorum et Architectorum* by Andrea Pozzo (1642–1709). Pozzo was a Jesuit priest, painter, architect, mathematician and scenographer, as well as a master of optical illusions, able to conjure up imaginary scenes. His prolific output had a tremendous influence on architects throughout Europe.

During the 17th century, artists built on and developed the lessons of Renaissance perspective; harnessing illusion to impress the onlooker, creating imaginary

Dome of the Chapel del Rosario, 1649–1690, Puebla, Mexico
Every single architectural element has been heavily decorated almost to the point of becoming unrecognisable. Each rib of the dome carries a divine image; there is an angel in the pendentive above the window, while the rest of the surface is encrusted with stuccoes, polychrome and gilded ornamentation. Drawn from 15th and 16th century Spanish Plateresque tradition, (meaning 'in the manner of a silversmith'), the skilful and complex decoration was freely employed in many churches as well as in the Spanish colonies, in Central and South America.

spaces that seemed to expand interiors and to blur built boundaries. This illusory technique was used in depictions of divine and spiritual glorification, church cupolas were adorned with illuminated clouds that seemed to rise up into the sky in a spiral of light, as if triumphing over the two-dimensional plasterwork surface itself. Artifice was not entirely masked, however, because if the illusion was not revealed in some way and it had been too convincing, it would have been incapable of causing the amazement that was intended in the first instance, making the whole exercise pointless. Trompe l'œil frescoes were therefore executed in such a way that by moving further away from the ideal vantage point, the artifice would be exposed and its illusion destroyed.

below, left
Francesco Borromini, gallery, Palazzo Spada, 1656–1660, Rome
The apertures in this small gallery allow light to suffuse the space and were used as a device by Borromini in order to articulate the space. Light is thus used as part of the perspectival trickery, creating an optical illusion that convinces the onlooker that the gallery is far longer than it actually is. The diminishing rows of columns and coffered ceilings add to the elongating effect, making the arcade's 8.6 metres seem more like four times that length.

below, right
Domenico Valmagini, Ferdinando Galli da Bibiena, dome of the Church of San Cristoforo, 1687, Piacenza
This simple dome is decorated with trompe l'œil, (a French term used to describe paintings that create optical illusions through realistic depictions). In this case, a second building has been depicted to emphasise the effect of the upward thrust of the dome.

PIAZZAS AS URBAN BACKDROPS

Piazzas were built with flamboyance, were magnificently decorated and treated rather like internal spaces. Given their scale and prominence, piazzas were well suited places to convey power, creating the perfect venue for gathering the population in one public space.

Triumphal arches were erected and lavish façades applied to palaces and churches in order to host the major festivities in Rome, such as those for the Jubilee or papal investitures. These interventions often obscured the true appearance of the city.

Gradually, various fixed embellishments began to supplant temporary ones and designs for urban and architectural interventions took on a decidedly theatrical character. Cities became more lavish, displaying their architecture, their piazzas and their thoroughfares in an effort to impress.

The design for the Piazza dei Quattro Canti in Palermo (later used for the reconstruction of Catania after an earthquake) was driven by the desire to remind the population of who held the reigns of power. Thus a permanent and opulent open-air theatre was constructed. The Palazzata (1622–1624, subsequently destroyed), known as the 'great marine theatre' was a uniform, monumental, continuous series of palaces built along the seafront in Messina. A similar development was built in Sicily.

This dramatic series of private buildings followed the natural curve of the bay, creating a backdrop quite unlike the traditional image of naval fortifications.

Giulio Lasso, Mariano Smeriglio, Giovanni De Avanzato, view from the Piazza dei Quattro Canti, 1609–1623, Palermo

During the early 17th century, a cruciform street layout, created by the intersection of the Cassero and Via Maqueda, was employed to reaffirm Palermo's image as a capital city. The city was thus split into four districts and four buildings were built on the corner junctions of each block. Concave façades overlook the square, thus creating a kind of circular open-air communal living space. The architectural vocabulary was inspired by the Piazza delle Quattro Fontane in Rome; it was highly grandiose — so sensational that it was dubbed the 'Theatre of the Sun'. Each façade consists of three superimposed orders with a water feature held in the bottom section. The upper levels are embellished with niches containing statues of the patron saints of each *mandamento* (district), the Spanish viceroys in Sicily and the four seasons.

BAROQUE CHURCHES

The Counter-Reformation heralded a move from the central plan of the Renaissance (a Humanist symbol of perfection) in sacred architecture, to basilicas designed in the form of a Latin cross. This plan layout originated in the Middle Ages and was characterised by an elongated longitudinal nave. The long nave had in fact proved to be more suited to the new liturgical requirements, which prescribed a broad space that could accommodate larger congregations and could focus greater attention on the altar.

Towards the latter part of the 16th century, Jesuits advocated that the church of Il Gesù in Rome be used as a prototypical model of a perfect blend of liturgical functionality and formal austerity. Il Gesù was to be replicated numerous times in churches throughout Italy as well as in other Catholic countries between 1600 and 1760. Thus their superficial decor became ever more lavishly decorative in the new aesthetic style. The search for typological integration continued, and gradually the relationship between churches and the urban fabric surrounding them was transformed. The longitudinal axis, accentuated by the late 16th century architectural form, was introduced — inward looking and independent. Church façades became plastic elements, demarcating the interface from sacred interior to sacral exterior space. Eventually architecture of the 17th century began to focus on the vertical axis, thus it is logical that experiments on domes were some of the most interesting performed during the Italian and European Baroque epoch.

Attempts at emphasising the longitudinal axis without detracting from the majestic and definitive perfection of the central space, led to many interesting solutions to the design of domes.

below, left
Carlo Maderno, Santa Susanna, 1603, Rome
Santa Susanna is often said to be the first true piece of Baroque architecture. Although the façade remains largely faithful to Renaissance principles with two superimposed orders, its dynamically enlivened composition is completely original. The gradual contraction of the spaces and the increasing plasticity of the elements as they move closer to the central axis, provide astonishing chiaroscuro effects and formal tension, as the side pilasters give way to engaged columns, three-quarter detached columns as well as complete freestanding columns.

below, right
Giacomo della Porta, Carlo Maderno, Altar, Sant'Andrea della Valle, 1590–1650, Rome
The main innovation in the interior of Sant'Andrea della Valle is the manner in which the elements and the spaces are integrated vertically: the pilasters continue beyond the trabeation (a well-defined horizontal element, similar to a cornice) extending into the transversal ribs of the vault over the nave and the apse at the rear of the building. Thanks to the plasticity of its constituent parts and the dynamic play of light, the interior is an open, endlessly transforming space in stark contrast to the traditional, static buildings of the Renaissance era.

The earliest trials consisted of the straightforward combination of the horizontal and vertical axes, usually achieved by creating a fairly short, broad nave and a relatively reduced transept, placing the focus on the central space of the dome. The effect was still fairly primitive and single elements were added that failed to integrate and become an organic part of the structure. Over time however, individual elements and separate spaces became less autonomous and – in line with Baroque principles – began to play an integral part in creating harmonious structures.

Experiments in northern Italy contributed enormously to achieve this concept of the interpenetration of spaces. In both Milan and Venice, churches were built according to plans where the optical effect of depth was achieved by the use of two succeeding centrally-planned spaces enclosed by a dome. The vertical surfaces of the two spaces were united visually by the repetition of vertical and horizontal elements.

Central plans were deemed to be pagan: first the Tridentine Council and then Carlo Borromeo, Archbishop of Milan (*Instructions on Church Building*, 1572) exhorted a return to the Latin cross plan. Notwithstanding this, central plans continued to be popular throughout the entire Baroque era. Firstly, this was a solution best suited to the new architectural demands for plastic and spatial integration; furthermore circular plans allowed vertical axes to be emphasised, sparking new dynamic relationships, also with the urban fabric surrounding them.

Longitudinal plans were conducive to elongation and central plans to centralisation. The dynamism and contraction of Baroque spatial principles thus led to the

below, left
Francesco Maria Richini, choir, Church of San Giuseppe, 1607–1630, Milan
San Giuseppe embodies a brilliant combination of two centrally-planned spaces of varying heights. The first space is octagonal and corresponds to the former nave, while the second, the presbytery, (a space reserved for officiating clergy, around the main altar) is situated on a square base with a cruciform layout. The polychrome marble floor dates back to the year 1644; the spatial autonomy of each space is demarcated by various geometric designs. In elevation, the two volumes are skilfully united by a common composite order and a uniform, unbroken wall plane.

below, right
François Mansart, plan for the church of St Marie de la Visitation, 1632–1634, Paris
The initial design for this church was a far simpler shape (circle) but was then embellished with the addition of large side chapels (1), open along the two main axes and accessible via narrow, slightly undulating steps and smaller, blind chapels (2) along the diagonal axes. The main chapels are linked to the central space (3) in a completely original manner: rather than being added as independent volumes they partly intersect with the circular space.

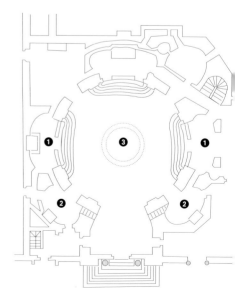

circle being transformed into an elliptical shape. Previously introduced by Vignola in the mid-to-late 16th century, elongated oval plan layouts with domes were to become one of the most popular and successful solutions in 17th and 18th century European architecture.

In France, for example, central plans were popular because they conformed to local Classical taste, however the ellipse also enjoyed some success and was employed for grand salons or for atriums of castles and noble buildings more frequently than for churches. Bernini explored this particular device extensively during his career, employing both the simple shape of the circle; as in the church of the Assunta at Ariccia (directly inspired by the Pantheon) and the oval shape in one of his greatest works, the church of Sant'Andrea al Quirinale.

Pietro da Cortona, façade, Church of St Luca e Martina, 1635–1650, Rome
The mighty, yet elegant dome rises up behind the façade to tower over the city. The outer walls complement the interior spaces and the curvature of the façade reflects the semicircular curve of the entrance space.

STAIRCASES

The most significant 17th century examples of staircases are to be found primarily in large Italian cities like Genoa, Naples, Venice and Milan.

The most creative solutions were generated in urban contexts where the buildings were densely packed and the streets narrow. In Genoa and the capital of the Spanish colonial empire, Mexico City, the building of enormous palaces with large courtyards tended to be challenging. In order to bestow elegance and prestige to buildings, architects focused on individual, particularly distinctive features, such as portals, entrances and stairways.

Italian staircases built in the 17th century were often based on Spanish 16th century models; especially on the so-called 'Imperial Staircase'.

The first Imperial Staircases were built at the Escorial in Madrid and the Alcázar in Toledo, after which the vogue took off rapidly throughout Europe (e.g. the Ambassadors' Stair at Versailles). The Imperial Staircase consists of an open staircase inscribed in a rectangular space, where a single-carriage flight leads to a landing, where it divides into two separate carriages – parallel with the first flight – leading to the floor above. These staircases tend to have balustrades on the far side that allow in high levels of light to penetrate into the space. They are characterised by their monumentality, transparency and luminosity.

below, left
Cosimo Fanzago, atrium and staircase at San Giuseppe a Pontecorvo, 1643–1660, Naples
A double-carriage staircase rises from a magnificent, well-lit atrium; the two separate branches converge to lead to the nave which sits above street level. This is a particularly creative and original solution. Fanzago may well have drawn on 16th century Genoese/Lombard architectural traditions.

below, right
Bartolomeo Bianco, Atrium and staircase at the Palazzo del Collegio dei Gesuiti (now part of the University), 1634–1636, Genoa
Bianco designed this highly classical building in Genoa, adapting it to suit the uneven topography with coherence and spatial continuity. He achieved this by creating a succession of open loggias, lofty staircases and dynamic perspectival views, bringing movement to the circulation spaces and conferring an impression of transparency and lightness.

THEATRES

Interest in the theatre burgeoned in Europe during the 17th century, with Italian plays and melodrama being especially favoured. The idea of constructing fixed stage sets – rather than the temporary structures used hitherto – developed quickly and they were built at the major royal courts. This was an ideal opportunity for Baroque to find its fullest expression, radically transforming dramatic art and laying the foundations for modern theatre. The greatest 17th century innovations concerned perspective, music, acoustics and plan layouts of auditoriums; scenic apparatus and backdrops were also developed. The Bibiena family was particularly active in this sphere, designing several European theatres, such as the Court Theatre in Vienna (1704). Their theories were disseminated throughout Europe thanks to the publication of their treatises on civilian architecture, which dealt with geometry and perspective. It was the Bibienas, for example, who first conceived the 'bell-shaped' plan, with an enclosed royal box surrounded by several rows of tiers. Baroque explorations of perspectival studies altered the relationship between the stage and the audience and established that the best view was to be had from the centre of the first row of tiers: thus the royal box, embellished with grandiose decorations, was positioned directly in front of the stage. Giacomo Torelli (1608–1678), an engineer and master of perspectival theory, developed seminal technical techniques, such as equipment for moving the side wings and fast changes of scenery.

below, left
Bibiena family, scenographic study, late 17th/early 18th century
The Galli family came from Bibiena (Bologna) executing a great many stage sets for theatrical works, which were preserved as models for later productions. This drawing illustrates the principle of seeing things 'from an angle,' a concept that involved arranging the visual axes of stage sets diagonally, enabling the audience to become more intimately involved in the proceedings on-stage.

below, right
Giovanni Battista Aleotti, Farnese Theatre, Palazzo della Pilotta, 1617–1619, Parma
The 1956 reconstruction, based on the original drawings, brought the largest and most avant-garde 17th century Italian performance space back to life. The enormous space consists of a U-shaped seating arrangement with fourteen tiers. Originally, special ducal seating would have formed the centrepiece, a precursor to the 'royal box', a feature that would become common to most European theatres. The stage is forty metres long, while the Classical proscenium would have contained niches embellished with stucco statues.

THE BAROQUE GARDEN

Italian 17th century gardens were a natural evolution from 16th century Italian gardens, with their medieval-like enclosed, constricted spaces. The gardens were planned according to Humanist tenets, which dictated order through rationality. Architecture took absolute priority and therefore palaces dominated everything else: nature itself became architecture, the botanical elements being reduced to geometric shapes, 'tamed' by humans. Subsequent to the Mannerist transition, which was characterised by licence and caprice, 17th century gardens became places where mystery and magic replaced perfection and balance. Baroque gardens brought together several different places and were a representation of infinite space.

top
Pietro da Cortona, engraving of Villa Sacchetti al Pigneto, 1761, Rome
Only a few ruins remain of this suburban villa, designed by Pietro da Cortona. The nymphaeum, preceded by a loggia, was originally built in 1638, while the semicircular niches on either side of the country house were later additions. These niches led to two loggias that curved gently round to connect to the main façade. Although the building was relatively small, the visual effect must have been stunning, thanks to the play of curves and the lavishly decorated central exedra with its echoes of Antique architecture. The surrounding area was adorned with fountains, staircases, water features and statues.

bottom
Giacomo della Porta, Domenico Fontana, Giovanni Vasanzio and Carlo Maderno, water spectacle at Villa Aldobrandini, 1602–1621, Frascati, Rome
The extensive vista stretches from the exedra of the water spectacle, to the rear of the palace, into infinity. The magnificent park blends the garden seamlessly with the surrounding landscape. Water played a fundamental part in the overall composition with splendid waterfalls, fountains and canals creating accents in the gardens.

Thus they were designed to provide the onlooker with unexpected surprises. Architectural features fused with the natural ones, creating flamboyant large, open spaces, with pathways and visual axes that were no longer entirely governed by human perspective. As one retreated from the immediate vicinity of the palace, with its surrounding formal, geometric flower-beds and terraces, forms became more freeform and sinuous. A sequence of perspectival views defined the natural surroundings. In this sense, gardens became more like parks, opening outwards and becoming visually united with the surrounding territory. Italian 17th century gardens remained deeply influenced by the gardens of the Renaissance in terms of appearance; they also lay the foundation for the great French gardens.

Carlo Fontana, Isola Bella, 1632, Lake Maggiore
Although Villa Borromeo was built at different stages by different generations of architects, the buildings and gardens were conceived as a single unified work.
Carlo Fontana transformed what, until 1630, had been a simple fishing village on an island, into what appeared to be a floating garden, dominated by a monumental palace with dramatically laid out gardens over ten elegant, planted terraces, embellished with water basins, fountains, architectural features and a multitude of allegorical statues.

ROME: THE BIRTH OF BAROQUE

After the Council of Trent (1545–1563), the Roman Catholic Church — having successfully survived the difficult and austere Counter Reformation period — entrusted artists with the task of displaying their victory over Protestantism. Italian Baroque art was therefore dependent on the Church as a patron and given the task of communicating a triumphant image of Catholicism to the faithful to conceal what was in fact a time of deep social and economic crisis. Baroque works are often described as being rhetorical, as their vocabulary was sumptuous and their decoration sublime, geared to rousing the emotions of the onlooker in a suggestive and dramatic manner, thus convincing them of their absolute truth. It is worth noting that the clergy played an active role in political and cultural life during this period and wielded tremendous influence over the social consciences of the population. Between 1560 and 1660 many religious buildings were constructed all over Italy, numerous older churches were also redecorated or restored according the new trends. Restoration tended to be undertaken on ancient basilicas of some importance, not only as an architectural statement, but also as proof of the undiminished sovereignty of Catholicism over Protestantism that was devoid of history.

During the Counter Reformation, even the newly established religious orders (such as the Jesuits, the Theatines and the Barnabites) spent vast sums of money and employed leading architects to build new churches, thus becoming highly influential in the transformation of the city of Rome into a symbol of Catholicism.

Santa Maria in Montesanto, 1662–1679,
and Santa Maria dei Miracoli, 1661,
Piazza del Popolo, Rome

Francesco Borromini, view of the interior of San Giovanni in Laterano, 1646–1649, Rome

Borromini's restoration of the great 4th century AD Paleo-christian basilica, showed the utmost respect for the original building. In order to reinforce the structure of the building while attempting to give it a contemporary look, he paired the columns in the nave, enclosing them in broad piers, linked by monumental, classically rhythmic arches. Each pier is allocated a niche between two enormous pilasters, containing an aedicule in coloured marble, with a statue of one of the Apostles. The roof could not be rebuilt because of the enormous expense; the coffered ceiling dates back to the 16th century.

opposite page
Carlo Maderno, façade of St Peter's, Vatican City, 1607–1614,

During the years spanning across the turn of the 16th and 17th century, Pope Paul V commissioned one of the leading architects of the period to carry out his most prestigious commission; namely the completion of the façade of St Peter's. The Counter Reformation regulations held fast – even for Michelangel – forcing Maderno to alter the floor layout from a central, to a longitudinal plan by the addition of three bays. Madarno showed enormous sensitivity towards his great predecessor, unfortunately his solution for the façade (featuring a giant order) was nevertheless not very successful. His design destroyed the dynamic and chiaroscuro effects negating the dominant character of the cupola in particular. It was not until Bernini built the colonnade, that the original spectacular effect was restored.

The religious orders were not only responsible for the dissemination of Catholicism, along with their own ecclesiastical groups in Italy, Europe and the New World, they were also in charge of a great many civilian organisations, such as schools, hospitals and orphanages. Given that these religious brotherhoods were essentially proselytizing, they preferred simple, unadorned buildings which guaranteed maximum functionality and ease of construction, dovetailing symbolically with their moral principles of sobriety and rectitude.

By the late 16th century, Rome was once again the most powerful city in Europe. The brief, but significant reign of Pope Sixtus V (1585–1590) led to a new approach to the conception of urban spaces, based on new axial streets and wide straight roads that were intended to simplify the complexity of the medieval street plan.

Domenico Fontana (1543–1607) played a vital role in the development of the new urban layout which transformed the city into an orderly network of links between several centres, buildings and piazzas. Unlike before, the city was no longer focused around one main centre (such as the cathedrals during the Middle Ages), but was rather based on the monumental perspective and layout of the streets and piazzas. The main basilicas, as well as other prestigious Renaissance and historic buildings, became conceptual and visual points of reference. The main arterial roads were marked by ancient obelisks that frequently also demarcated axes for junctions and perspectival vanishing points. The myriad of public fountains built after the new city aqueduct also served the same purpose as focal points. The building programme in Rome focused primarily on churches and ecclesiastical buildings. It can be said that the civic identity of the glorified 'holy city' was slowly undermined over time (as was the case in other Baroque Italian cities, such as Naples).

It was not only paintings and sculpture that were dramatized during the Baroque, but every urban and architectural endeavour, including furniture design and interior decoration. Baroque spaces were designed to amaze, they required an arena, adequate lighting and, of course, an audience. Above all else, artists and designers avoided creating static pieces.

The major challenge for artists was try and bring architecture to life, as if designing a stage set, using undulating lines and setting up dynamic relationships between open and closed volumes; creating tensions and forces between the individual elements. Architects organised spatial sequences like a series of backdrops

Pietro da Cortona, Santa Maria della Pace, 1657, Rome
Whereas the lower order has a portico that projects extensively and the paired travertine columns set up a dynamic rhythm (convex-concave and light-shade), the upper order is slightly convex and is set further back. The framing of the lateral piers and the upward thrust of the powerful pediment are typical examples of the tension of Baroque architecture. By building a portico that protrudes out into the piazza and an upper floor that demarcates the boundary of the church, Cortona managed to achieve a wonderful effect of spatial depth, so that anyone who enters the piazza has the impression that they have already entered into an internal space. The church appears to be embraced by two enclosing wings that hold it and also link it to the surrounding area.

to the main focus, creating *vedute* (forced perspectives) for the onlooker with various viewpoints, altering the perspective and the forms with it. The play of light along the gold, marble and stucco surfaces animated the object under observation. Just as the 17th century theatres had brought the audience closer to the stage, the relationships between building and piazza was also altered. A kind of 'antechamber' or threshold was created to act as an interface between interior and exterior. Examples of this are St Peter's (the circular piazza held in colonnaded arms prepares the visitor for entering the church) and equally the projecting colonnades of Santa Maria della Pace and Sant'Andrea al Quirinale. Buildings were no longer limited to the confines of their perimeter walls but were drawn outwards in an extension of the curved flanking walls that seem to stretch into infinity.

The Barberini Family in Rome (1623–1644)

Thanks to Bernini's close relationship with Pope Urban VIII (Maffeo Barberini), he became the artist favoured to convey the glories of the papal family. Other leading architects of the time were Maderno, Borromini and da Cortona, who all worked in the courtyard at Palazzo Barberini, a sumptuous and original residence that was to change the face of architecture for ever.

Urban VIII is a good example of the powerful social contrasts of the time. During his reign, the pontificate had no qualms about diverting public funds towards the coffers of his own family. This obviously irked his dissatisfied inferiors, who were forced to silently witness the fraudulent gains and privileges enjoyed by the noblemen and clergy, while the rest of the population lived a life of deprivation.

As a response to the general climate of unrest, the pope revived old traditions, such as public holidays, hunting and theatre spectacles; customs that had all been cast aside during the Inquisition and the Counter Reformation. The pope initiated some major building works (both civil and military), commissioning leading architects of the period. These projects were controversial and many ancient monuments were damaged during the execution of these works, for instance, the bronze statues in the Pantheon were melted down and reused for the cannon at Castel Sant'Angelo and the ceiling in St Peter's, while marbles from the Colosseum were looted and ended up adorning Roman palaces. Hence the motto *Quod non fecerunt Barbari, fecerunt Barberini,* translated as, 'What the barbarians failed to do, the Barberini did.'

The Pamphili Family in Rome (1644–1655)

The Peace of Westphalia (1648) brought the bloody Thirty Years' War to an end during the reign of Pope Innocent X, (born Giambattista Pamphili). Another major event of the time was undoubtedly the 1650 Jubilee, when some 700,000 pilgrims, including Queen Cristina of Sweden, descended en masse on Rome. Classical monuments were restored and many other building projects were executed in honour of the occasion, while the Pontiff surrounded himself with the most talented artists of the generation. In fact, when the Pope took over power, he criticised the achievements of his predecessor, Pope Urban VIII and — for political rea-

Eastern elevation of Palazzo Barberini, 1626, Rome
The original compact Renaissance block with its central courtyard was converted, as a more complex articulation of the spaces was desired. During the 17th century, architects were mindful of the impact that large-scale Roman residential palaces and enormous churches would have on the urban environment around them. The short wings on either side of the main building illustrate the desire to forge a closer relationship between the building and the city. The wide entrance portal – with seven arches on all three floors – acts a filter between the interior and the exterior, as if to invite the public to share its grandiosity. Given the palazzo's location – near the gardens on the-then outskirts of Rome – the palazzo must have seemed like a monumental rural villa, reminiscent of the typical Renaissance relationship between villa and nature.

sons no doubt — his reign was not a fruitful time for Bernini, the Barberini's favourite artist. Almost as a direct consequence of this — given the famous rivalry between the two artists — Pope Innocent X became Borromini's main patron. The pontiff was not a Humanist, nor was he particularly enamoured with literature or the arts. He did however, have a keen interest in architecture; partaking in the recommencement of building works on Palazzo Nuovo on Piazza del Campidoglio as well as the construction of the Prison Nuove. Aside from this, his attention was focused on Piazza Navona, the site he had earmarked as being eminently suitable for the glorification of his family.

opposite page
Piazza Navona, 1647, Rome
This beautiful ancient piazza is built on the former site of the Stadium of Domitian (1st century AD) and became the hub of 17th century Roman public life. The walls of the buildings that enclose the piazza are continuous, making the piazza seem like an extension of their interiors; rather like an open-air salon. The 17th century scheme focused on Palazzo Pamphili and on the church of Sant' Agnese in Agone, situated in the centre of the piazza. When Borromini designed the concave façade of the church, his intention was to try and create an intimate relationship between the church and the piazza onto which it opened. He designed the building to embrace the piazza, its wings culminating in two lantern towers. The piazza hosted jousts and festivals, accommodating every kind of public event. The piazza contains three fountains, all positioned along the same axis: the two side fountains occupy the centre of an ellipse. The famous, Fontana dei Fiumi (Fountain of the Four Rivers) and the Fontana del Moro (Fountain of the Moor) were both designed by Bernini.

Francesco Borromini, view of the dome cladding and bell-tower of Sant'Andrea delle Fratte, 1653, Rome
The church was not completed in Borromini's time, however had the architect completed it, he would most likely have covered the brickwork of the tiburio (dome cladding) with stucco in order to tie it in with the bell-tower. Borromini devoted his research to the study of the relationship between these two elements; dome and bell-tower. He moved the bell-tower from the façade and replaced it alongside the dome. Thus the tower was given a more prominent position and could act as a landmark. The close proximity of the bell-tower to the dome meant that it shifted and changed according to the perspective at which it was viewed.

BERNINI THE ARCHITECT

Bernini did not become an architect until his later years, during the reign of Pope Alexander VII Chigi. Initially he was a sculptor and painter and did not embark on architectural projects until his mature years. His only involvement at a young age was with Palazzo Barberini at Arriccia and Castel Gandolfo, both built to a central plan. After three decades, i.e. after Maffeo Barberini's papacy had ceased, Rome had a Humanist pope once more namely, Pope Alexander VII. Pope Alexander enjoyed studying philosophy and wrote poems in Latin; surrounding himself with the leading artists and architects of the time. Apart from Bernini, his young assistant, Carlo Fontana, Rainaldi and Borromini were the undisputed protagonists of what the Pope regarded as the rebirth of Rome. Gripped by a frantic desire to build, the Pope invested vast quantities of pontifical money into the construction of the city, in a quest to elevate Rome to the league of Ancient Rome. Bernini had a large number of streets widened, thereby destroying old, existing homes, remodelling piazzas to confer an air of majesty and antiquity, as was the case of Piazza del Popolo. Bernini was placed in charge of St Peter's and the great schemes for St Peter's Piazza. During this period Bernini also built Palazzo Montecitorio and Sant'Andrea al Quirinale, these projects gave him the opportunity to revisit the typology of centrally-planned churches.

below, left
Gian Lorenzo Bernini, Sant'Andrea al Quirinale, 1658–1670, Rome
The church, with its gigantic pediment, has an imposing flat façade. The concave side wings are mirrored on the interior of the building and the semicircular portico faces onto the square, thus giving the impression of the building pressing outwards.

below, right
Gian Lorenzo Bernini, Scala Regia in the Vatican, 1663–1666, Vatican City
Bernini arranged the columns in the lower part of the staircase in the Vatican in order to alter the perspective and make the walls seem more regular. The architect divided the steps into two flights from the landing and lit them by concealed side lighting.

The urban image of 17th century Rome was largely defined by its religious architecture, commissioned by popes or religious orders. Public works were predominantly geared to the alteration and to the building of new streets, bridges and fountains, whilst not much civil building was undertaken. The 'holy city' had in fact absorbed the bulk of the budget for renewal and kept many leading artists employed. Even the aristocratic palaces tended to be commissioned by the papal families. Palazzo Montecitorio was built for the Pamphili family while Pope Innocent X was in power and Alexander VII continued the trend by commissioning several noble residential palaces, including Palazzo Chigi in Piazza Santi Apostoli (Palazzo Chigi Odescalchi, 1665–1667). Here Bernini designed a building with a monumental façade and Classical forms, decorating it with giant orders of pilasters on the *piano-nobile* and the second floors, above the ground floor plinth. Bernini also utilised this design, (which resembled that for Palazzo Montecitorio), in his designs for the Palais du Louvre.

Gian Lorenzo Bernini, Palazzo Montecitorio, 1650–late 17th century, Rome
Despite its austerity and simplicity, the articulation of this monumental façade is emphatically Baroque: the slightly convex nature of the surfaces and the opening out of the wings flanking the building testify to a 17th century approach to urban space. The symmetrical façade is made up of five different sections that culminate in a projecting central section; its edges demarcated by slightly protruding, full-height piers. The architectural symmetry is held by the splendid portal that marks the central axis. Building work ground to a halt after the ground floor was completed in 1655 and was eventually completed by Fontana towards the turn of the century, with only a few modifications to the original design.

FRANCESCO BORROMINI

Originally a stonemason from Lombardy, Francesco Borromini worked in the building yard at the Duomo in Milan, only moving to Rome later, in around 1614. He began his career as a marble engraver, working on St Peter's cathedral under Carlo Maderno. Borromini's most significant architectural commissions came from minor patrons, such as brotherhoods and religious orders, whilst he only enjoyed the favour of the Pontifical Court on occasion. He had the reputation of being an introverted and difficult man, in some respects rather like the infamous painter, Caravaggio. Apparently he frequently quarrelled with Bernini, who was the antithesis if him and who is said to have accused Borromini of 'basing his proportions on fantasy,' and harshly stated that he had been sent 'to destroy architecture.' In actual fact Borromini was inspired by nature and nature's complex geometry. He was also influenced by Michelangelo's rebellious interpretation of classical codes; thus rejecting the concept of architecture as a reflection of the proportions of the human body, but rather looking to Antiquity for inspiration. His works resonate with echoes of past styles; not merely as imitations but rather as transformations captured by his incredible sensitivity, idiosyncrasy and brilliant creative powers. The oriental influence of his work and naturalistic expression of his architecture would undoubtedly have perplexed his contemporaries.

Francesco Borromini, façade of the oratory and the Casa dei Filippini, 1637–1640, Rome
The oratory was the first curved façade to be built in Rome. According to Borromini, it was inspired by the human body with its wings outstretched like arms to welcome visitors. The undulating movement of the façade gives the impression of the elevation folding back on itself. The building seems to be alive, like a living organism. The use of perfectly aligned bricks (an Ancient Roman technique), creating a finely woven, textured surface, accentuates this impression.

THE MASTERPIECE
SANT'IVO ALLA SAPIENZA

Borromini was commissioned to build a church within the existing cloister of the Archiginnasio. The challenge of Borromini's task lay in trying to design the scheme in the constricted site, however he managed to rise to the challenge by conceiving a brilliant centrally-planned church, which was arguably his greatest work. His contemporaries were evidently overwhelmed by the genius of his solution and the eccentric shape of the lantern that he had designed. They did not recognise any traditional architectural references in the geometry or in the relationships and shapes, regarding his design as a preposterous attempt to break the boundaries of form and space. In actual fact, there were many references to Antique architecture; Borromini had simply reformulated them into a creative vocabulary of his own, which was not immediately identifiable. One assumes that the architect would never have stooped to mere imitation of past styles.

The rigorous geometric and mathematical theories underpinning his design were influenced by the great many scientific discoveries of the 17th century — the era of Galileo. The scientist propounded that the universe was based on mathematical principles; a theory that was strenuously refuted by Pope Urban VII and professors from the university.

opposite page
Francesco Borromini, view from the west side of Sant'Ivo alla Sapienza, 1642–1660, Rome
The courtyard of Sant'Ivo alla Sapienza was built by the architects, Pirro Ligorio and Giacomo della Porta in 1632, at the same time as the university building in 1578 was altered by Borromini. The concave curve of the façade is the inverse of the drum above it. The curved elevation contains one side of the courtyard and is so perfectly interlinked with it that the two are seamlessly intertwined as a single entity. The courtyard is enclosed on the remaining three sides by a double-storey colonnade, which draws the eye towards the church. The façade of the church is articulated by pilasters and arched windows that also serve to emphasise the overall visual continuity. The coat of arms of the Chigi family adorns either side of the curving façade.

above
Francesco Borromini, interior view of the dome of Sant'Ivo alla Sapienza, 1642–1660, Rome
The cupola of the church sits directly on the cornice. The six golden sections of the drum spring from the edges of the cornice and terminate at the impost ring of the lantern. Thus, vertical continuity is achieved, with the form of the floor plan echoed in the cupola.

BAROQUE IN ITALY

Beyond Rome, the remainder of Italy was rather more reluctant to embrace Baroque. Cities that had previously been at the forefront of artistic fervour saw a slowing down in construction due to epidemics and general economic decline. Florence was the most salient example of this slowdown: at the close of the Mannerist era, there was no obvious talent in the new generation of up-and-coming architects who would be able to compete with the achievements of the former masters. As a consequence of this, one of the key artistic hubs of Europe slid into architectural obscurity, despite the fact that Baroque had initially taken root in Medici Florence. It had been Michelangelo's vestibule in the Laurenziana Library in Florence that had unnerved his contemporaries with its proportions and lines that diverted from Classical canons.

Gabriele Riccardi, view of the dome
di Santa Croce, 1590, Lecce

The second major centre of Italian Baroque was indisputably Turin. The Savoia family had kept a tight reign on activities in Rome and Paris and had used architecture and urban planning as a means of symbolising their absolute power. The Savoias sought the expertise of one of the major architects of the period, Guarino Guarini, who happened to have spent time in Turin during his many travels. It was in Turin that Guarini executed some of his most successful work and where he laid the foundation for the grand developments of the 18th century. Elsewhere in Italy there were only a few isolated cases of Baroque buildings in Northern Italy, but none triggered subsequent developments. The Republic of Venice was noteworthy as the city had ambitions to affirm its international standing on the mercantile and political stage. Venice aimed to develop an image to rival that of Rome, which the Venetians were not prepared to recognise as the capital of Catholicism. Thus the celebratory nature of the

opposite page
Ground floor capital at Santa Croce, 16th century, Lecce
The Baroque style that developed in Lecce contained a great many medieval adornments (animals, monsters, mermaids), drawn directly from 16th century architecture. Stylistic continuity was assured by the influence of traditional local craftsmanship and the use of tufa, which was very malleable, thus facilitating the crafting of sumptuous decorations, which became so intricate that the stone started to resemble embroidery.

Guarino Guarini, view of the cupola of San Lorenzo, 1668–1680, Turin
The original, complex internal structure cannot be detected from the exterior. Guarini's work undoubtedly focused on the interior, where the onlooker could cast their gaze upwards to be awestruck by the soaring heights. That said however, it is worth noting that the exterior of San Lorenzo was not built according to Guarini's plans. Turin's rulers were concerned that Guarini's idiosyncratic solutions would sully the city's image and jeopardise their precious balance of power: it was not in the interests of the nobility that a church should attract too much attention. Many typical Baroque characteristics can be seen in the lantern however, alternating concave-convex shapes as well as windows crowned by pairs of small columns. The rippling forms interact with the form of the underlying mass (the octagonal cupola) whilst the concentration of pilasters in the corners creates a similar formal tension.

new Baroque architecture found fertile ground in Venice, to profoundly influence a great many building projects.

Despite Baldassare Longhena's architectural brilliance, 16th century traditional principles still held fast in the lagoon city and architecture remained anchored in the local Classical Renaissance style, quashing any new trends. Generally speaking however, there was a certain amount of dabbling with the new spatiality of Baroque in Northern Italy, though expressed in a personalised manner developing largely independently of Rome. In cities like Venice, Milan and Genoa, variations to the central plan, as well as the buildings designed by Longhena, Richini and Bianco, were simultaneous to the great flurry of activity in Rome and developed independently from it.

In contrast, the development of Baroque in Southern Italy was being played out altogether differently. Rome had a far greater influence on the southern regions,

Mariano Smiriglio, Vincenzo La Barbera, Angelo Italia, dome of the church of the Carmine Maggiore, 1626, Palermo
The dome was a unique expression of Sicilian Baroque, quite unlike any other buildings either in Palermo or anywhere else in Sicily. The dome rests on a tall drum and appears to be supported by four gigantic supports standing between the columns. Enormous windows between the grotesque figures illuminate the interior. The frames of these huge windows are richly decorated with stucco and floral motifs. The dome is adorned with unusual multicoloured majolica and terminates in a vaulted lantern.

opposite page
Guarino Guarini, detail of the interior of the lantern in the Church of Sacra Sindone, 1667–1682, Turin
The lantern was designed in the form of a large twelve-point star with a dove at the centre, symbolising the Holy Spirit. Guarini managed to create a feeling of weightlessness and mysterious luminosity by puncturing the lantern with twelve, small, oval windows.

given that most of the Neapolitan architects had trained in Rome. Naples became a great Baroque urban centre relatively quickly, sparking a trend that spread rapidly throughout Southern Italy. There were several prominent architects who worked there, like Fanzago for instance, though their projects tended to lack individuality.

Baroque undoubtedly rose to its greatest heights in Southern Italy (though it was not until the 18th century that it truly burgeoned there), the experiments were more decorative than spatial.

BALDASSARE LONGHENA

Baldassare Longhena (1598–1682), a pupil of the sculptor Scamozzi, was a legendary figure. His greatest masterpiece was the church, Santa Maria della Salute, which he built well before any of the great buildings in Rome had been realised. The church was original and innovative; an excellent example of a regional and personal interpretation of Baroque set within the elongated urban plan of Venice. Unfortunately, after his death Longhena left no real successor and Venetian architects returned to the concept of Baroque as the natural evolution of 16th century architecture, while the penchant for Late Renaissance lingered. Giuseppe Sardi's (1630–1699) architecture epitomised this affinity. The fame Longhena achieved with Santa Maria della Salute, allowed him to springboard to the undisputed heights of 17th century Venetian architecture and consequently to be awarded many great commissions in Venice. Longhena worked furiously, designing and building convents, schools, churches and even palaces. Private clients, particularly from noble families, increasingly commissioned him. During the decade between 1640 and 1650, Longhena built a great many private palaces, most of them situated along the Grand Canal, these included: Palazzo Morosini on the gardens to San Canciano (1644), Palazzo Belloni Battagia on the Grand Canal at San Stae (1648) and a palace on the Grand Canal at San Barnaba (1649). All these *palazzi* contained powerful elements specific to the locality of Venice. Longhena often made reference to Sansovino's models in his private commissions and seldom made alterations to either the plans or the layout of the traditional noble Venetian residences, remaining faithful to the more traditional medieval methods. However, on the exterior façades Longhena reformulated the 16th century Venetian tenants into his own particular vocabulary, endowing his palaces with monumental form and scale that enabled the residences to flaunt the power and wealth of the aristocratic families who lived there.

Baldassarre Longhena, *Ca' Pesaro* view from the Grand Canal, 1659–1682, Venice
This noble palace on the Grand Canal was possibly the greatest expression of Longhena's ability to reinterpret the Baroque style into 'Venetian Baroque'. Despite the fact that the composition of the façade derives from Sanmicheli and from Sansovino's traditional 16th century solution for Palazzo Corner, there are also obvious Baroque characteristics like the plastic, sculptured treatment of the surfaces that sets up a rhythm of solids and voids and light and shadow typical of Baroque architecture.

THE MASTERPIECE
SANTA MARIA DELLA SALUTE

Santa Maria della Salute was the first building where a giant Palladian order was employed in a centrally-planned building. The composition of the façade, with a central triumphal arch, is repeated eight times on either side of the octagon. The church illustrates how Venetian tradition and Byzantine style can be blended with great visual cohesion. The dramatic effect is achieved using the picturesque device of employing two domes of different sizes (the smaller one cannot be seen on the photograph). The monumentality of this church must have radically altered the urban landscape of 17th century Venice.

Baldassarre Longhena, exterior view and detail of the façade of Santa Maria della Salute, 1631–1648, Venice
The larger cupola is adorned with sculptures and surrounded by twelve powerful buttresses formed like volutes and known as 'ears'. The buttresses are structural elements that are placed outside the building in order to counter the internal thrust of the vaults and arches. Longhena also attributed a symbolic meaning to the buttresses: by encircling the drum, they create a kind of crown dedicated to the Virgin Mary, to whom the church was dedicated as a votive offering for the city's deliverance from the plague that had engulfed it, (hence its name *la Salute* or 'health').

GUARINO GUARINI

Guarino Guarini (1624–1683) originally trained as a theologian and mathemati- cian and belonged to the Theatines, a religious order that commissioned him to design and build a great number of churches in a great many places, including Prague, Paris, Lisbon, Messina, Vicenza, as well as several other smaller Italian cities. In 1663, Guarini was summoned to Turin by the Duke of Savoy, Carlo Emanuele II. The majority of architects in Turin originated from Piedmont and had learned their trade in military construction. The arrival of the outsider, Guarini in Turin undoubtedly caused a stir, but fortunately the architects managed to har- ness the knowledge of Piedmont's engineering and the region's traditional passion for structural experimentation. It was in Turin that Guarini's greatest works found expression and were most appreciated. Despite the complex formal language of his architecture, his radical structural design was admired. The incredible vertical arrangements of his buildings sprung from brilliant plan layouts. Guarini organised space according to principles derived from nature: the spatial cells (as single spe- cial units) that demarcate his interiors are generated by the buildings' interwoven rhythm of expansion and contraction. This was a completely original process that had no relationship to the traditional development of spaces and was more like a fusion, where the cells cease to exist as autonomous entities and rather form part of an organic whole. Guarini had a similar approach to Borromini's, the architec- ture of which Guarini had admired during a visit to Rome. Both architects regarded architecture as an ensemble of space and light and, in this sense, their works sel- domly contained purely decorative Baroque elements. For both Guarini and Bor- romini geometry and space were the most important elements, neither architect was concerned with covering surfaces with decorations but rather sought to use their absence, thereby creating clean shapes and simple materials. By carving out the spaces held between the load-bearing structures (for example the masonry wall plane between piers), they pared the architecture down to its essence. Guar- ini even went so far as to omit the surfaces of his vaults, leaving nothing but the ribs, thereby enabling daylight to penetrate from several different angles. This 'skeleton' effect, where the surrounding fabric appears to dissolve, is reminiscent of Gothic churches. It is logical that one of Guarini's most interesting projects, with regard to this tracery of stone, was in the church of St-Anne-la-Royale (since destroyed) in Paris, which he designed during the time that French tradition of building in stone was at its zenith. Thanks to the boldness of his structural explo- rations, Guarini managed to achieve the extreme verticality of Gothic architecture. His buildings were so innovative that they attracted both fear and awe simultane- ously.

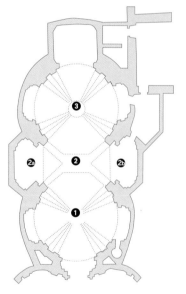

Guarino Guarini, ceiling and plan for the nave of the church of the Immacolata Concezione, 1673–1697, Turin
The church space is defined by a series of three elements that draw the eye towards the altar. Of the three separate units, the two outer ones are circular (1 and 3), whilst the central one is hexagonal (2). The elements are not simply juxtaposed alongside one another, but rather blend and interlink so masterfully that it is hard to con- ceive of them as being autonomous. The longitudinal axis is dominant, whilst the central unit (2) is the anti- thesis of the first as it has its own, transversal axis (2a/2b).
The tension between the two axes triggers the impression of the expansion and con- traction of the space, giving an impression of dynamic, pulsating movement.

THE MASTERPIECE
SAN LORENZO

Guarini took experimentation with vaulted domes to new heights in San Lorenzo. Here, the traditional solid cupola has been pierced with apertures to be flooded with light, leaving only the interwoven ribs exposed (1, axonometric drawing); recalling certain Late Gothic structures. Unlike Baroque architecture, Gothic regarded form and function as being inseparable: the architectural element, therefore had to correspond to the structural system, without any pastiche or architectural ploys. Baroque, on the other hand, was full of fictional devices.

Guarini astonished his contemporaries by being able to create voids where there ought to have been solids (e.g. side chapels carved out of the base of the piers that should have supported the cupola, 2, axonometric drawing), but unfortunately the structure proved to be inadequate. Therefore, in order to conceal his ploy, Guarini created a double structure: the visible one seems as if it is load-bearing, but in reality it only held up its own weight, while the true structure, which rested on the outer walls of the church, remained concealed.

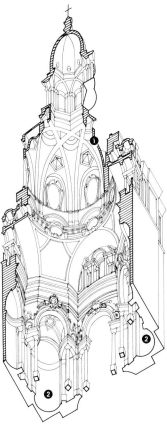

Guarino Guarini, view of the cupola and axonometric of San Lorenzo, 1668–1680, Turin

NAPLES

During the 17th century most of the cultural and civil activity in Southern Italy was linked to Naples, the capital of the Spanish Viceroy and a major trading hub. As from the early 17th century, Naples had already become one of the most densely populated cities in Europe, second only to Paris. This led to the remodelling of the urban fabric and renewed building activity, laying fertile ground for the evolution of Baroque. Naples epitomised the true Baroque Italian city, witnessed some of the best artistic triumphs in Italy and was where artists, like Caravaggio executed their finest works. In the architectural milieu, the new religious orders joined the ruling classes as patrons, which led to the building of over a hundred churches. The face of the city transformed into a metropolis, thereby altering the balance of religious and civil architecture. Baroque found its expression through the obsessive passion for decoration and the use of coloured materials — the fashion for polychrome marble ornamentation and 'marmo commesso' (intarsia), already widespread from the late 16th century, reached its peak during the 17th century. The architectural research being conducted in Rome during that period spread to nearby Naples, but failed to take root until the 17th century. Thus, Neapolitan Baroque remained tied to a provincial interpretation, expressed through decoration and pictorial effects, recognised as being the simplest and most efficient methods of religious persuasion; meanwhile, church plan layouts continued to feature the traditional nave with side chapels.

below, left
Francesco Grimaldi, Chapel of the Treasure of San Gennaro, 1608, Naples Cathedral
As well as being well known for housing the reliquary containing the blood of San Gennaro, the chapel is also known to epitomise 17th century Neapolitan Baroque. Most of the leading artists of the period were involved in the adornment of the church. The space houses a powerful concentration of highly valuable works of art within a small space.

opposite page, right
Cosimo Fanzago, interior of the
church at the Certosa di San Martino,
1623–1656, Naples
The Gothic architecture in San Martino
can still be detected in the ribbed
cross-vaults, while the rest of the surface is rendered unrecognisable due to
the tapestry of decoration that cover
the surfaces, consisting of marble
panels on the walls, polychrome floors,
stuccoes, sumptuous furnishings and
altars. The decor forms a harmonious
blend of 16th and 17th century taste.
The Certosa was Fanzago's first significant commission as an architect — he
embarked on an architectural career at
a late stage in his life, having reached
the peak of his fame as a sculptor and
stonemason. The interior of San Martino is an excellent example of Fanzago's great decorative ability in executing polychrome marble intarsia in
both imaginary and natural forms.

Giovan Antonio Dosio, Giacomo di
Conforto, Cosimo Fanzago, Main Cloister
(Chiostro Grande) of the Certosa di San
Martino, 1591–1631, Naples
The original design for this monumental monastery complex dates back to
the 14th century. The Certosa (consisting of the church, cloister and prior's
apartment) underwent various transformations between the late 16th and
the early 17th century. The interventions that best defined the Certosa di
San Martino stylistically, however were
those carried out during the 17th century by the scores of local artists involved in the project. From 1623 onwards,
Fanzago (1591–1678) worked on the
simple and harmonious architecture
of this cloister, which features a series
of arches set on marble columns,
embellishing Dosio's (1591–1609)
earlier work with sculptures, stucco
decorations and the splendid marble
baluster that forms the boundary of
the monks' cemetery.

LECCE

Thanks to a powerful religious class that intended to transform Lecce into a kind of church city, building during the 17th century was largely devoted to erecting sacred buildings. Bishop Luigi Pappacoda (1639–1670) spearheaded this renewal, intending to advance Lecce to a major centre of the Spanish Viceroy, second only to Naples. Baroque evolved within a cultural context that had been under the influence of Spain for a very long time and that still had strong links with the Middle Ages, given that the Renaissance caught on late there and was not very widespread. During the 17th century, artistic trends still reflected Romanesque, Norman and Mannerist influences. The new Roman and Neapolitan Baroque styles therefore shaped a personal and local vocabulary, still influenced by their rich cultural past, which was expressed through the great 'Salentino' artisan tradition.

Leccese Baroque, most famous for the work of Giuseppe Zimbalo (1617–1710), was characterised by great decorative exuberance, but never managed to evolve further than mere superficial embellishment (albeit extremely suggestive) and thus did not lead to full blown architectural and spatial experimentation. While Borromini and Guarini managed to play down the wall plane by detracting from its role as physical confine through the use of curved lines, the Leccese architects — like the Spanish and South American architects — created a similar effect (i.e. the nullification of the wall structure) by embellishing it with a profusion of ornamentation.

opposite page
View of the façade of Palazzo dei Celestini (former monastery), 1659–1695, Lecce
The palazzo dates from the second half of the 17th century and testifies to the affirmation of a more autonomous and personal style, a mature combination of the many influences of past, less Hispanic styles. The exterior is clad in fine rectangular rusticated blocks, articulated by barely projecting pilasters that are more markedly rusticated.
The volutes on the curved window spandrels on the first floor *piano nobile* (by Giuseppe Zimbalo) are testament to Fanzago's receptiveness to Neapolitan taste. When one compares the frames on the second order (late 17th century, by Giuseppe Cino), the move towards more sophisticated, typical Early Rococo shapes, is clearly evident.

Santa Croce, 1571–1646, Lecce
The façade of Santa Croce gives the impression of being a homogenous work carried out by one, single author though, in actual fact, it was built in several stages between the late 16th and the mid-17th century. The church is a supreme example of the Leccese Baroque style; its iconography has remained coherent over the centuries, representing the triumph of Christ over the infidels. The lower section, by Gabriele Riccardi, was built in the 16th century; whilst the balcony — supported by thirteen brackets in the shape of human figures symbolising the pagan world being quashed by the force of faith — dates back to the 17th century. The upper order is attributed to Cesare Penna and Giuseppe Zimbalo; it features a rose window flanked on either side by a statue of a saint and crowned with the coat of arms of the Celestines.

SICILY

In Sicily, which was also a part of the Spanish Viceroy, 17th century architecture was largely devoted to religious buildings. Within a short timespan many urban centres had adopted the Spanish monastic city model, as had been the case in Naples and Lecce. Sacred architecture, along with civil and military architecture, was largely confined to the island's main maritime hubs: Palermo and Messina. When Baroque tenants first caught on, architecture was still characterised by Norman influences, Late Mannerist remnants from Central Italy and, especially, trends largely driven by Spanish mores. From the mid-16th century onwards, new forms slowly began to emerge, largely thanks to the widespread activity of the Jesuit priests after the foundation of the church of Il Gesù in Palermo in 1564. Due to the devastation of the 1693 earthquake that almost completely destroyed eastern Sicily, the only Early Baroque remains that survive are to be found on the western part of the island. The 17th century reconstructions were conducted in a more mature and evolved style. Sicilian Baroque of the 17th century was an expression of high artistic quality, especially due to the skill of the artisans and the fruitful collaboration between sculptors and architects; it nevertheless remained a provincial vocabulary.

below
Giovanni Vermexio (most likely author), Palazzo del Senato, 1629–1633, Syracuse
Prior to the 19th century addition of the attic storey, the palazzo had been a perfect cube, divided horizontally by a long balcony. The orders, which are clearly separated, also differ in style: the lower order is typically Renaissance, elegant and harmonious, while the upper order is clearly Baroque; featuring grotesques, capitals decorated with shells, interrupted cornices and a variety of window surrounds. A large, carved Imperial eagle adorns the centre of the elevation. The upper cornice bears the signature of Vermexio (the architect from Syracuse who was of Spanish extraction), symbolised by a carved lizard that refers to his nickname, due to his alleged thinness.

above
View towards the altar of the Church of Il Gesù (or Casa Professa), 1564–1636, Palermo
Built by the Jesuits according to the Counter Reformation tenets of maximum simplicity, the Church of Il Gesù was substantially remodelled during the early 17th century. The typical nave and side chapels became a nave and two aisles, whilst the remains of the internal surfaces were completely covered with polychrome intarsia marble, frescoes and magnificent stuccoes (by Giacomo Serpotta). The apse exemplifies a harmonious blend of architectural and sculptural art, where the riot of colour and the precious materials succeed in amazing the onlooker.

right
Angelo Italia, interior of San Francesco Saverio, 1685–1711, Palermo
The enormous cupola of San Francesco Saverio is held by four smaller domes positioned over the hexagonal chapels. Each chapel is orientated towards the central space, opening on two different levels. The levels are separated by a kind of balcony that rests on columns which — together with the balconies of the other chapels — create the central octagon. The apertures in the drum of the central cupola, as well as those in the smaller domes, illuminate the church. The architect, Angelo Italia (1628–1700), opted for this plan layout in order to try and remodel sacred space, however his innovation failed to take root in Sicily.

THE SPREAD OF BAROQUE

Baroque art was recognised as a powerful representational tool for both political and religious power. As Baroque had taken root in the representation of sacred architecture in Rome, it spread and became popular throughout Europe, especially where the dukes and princes sought to reinvigorate the image of their cities through urban and architectural renewal. This renewal reached its zenith in the villas and noble palaces in France, where the nobility did everything in their power to flaunt their lofty positions. Though the spread of Baroque in France might not have been on a par with that in Italy, the projects that were built, such as Versailles and Le Nôtre's gardens, had an enormous influence on future developments that eventually led to the development of Rococo. Due to the flourishing trade in Europe, Protestant countries, such as Denmark and Sweden, for example, also played a role in spreading Baroque architecture. Sovereign monarchs were quick to employ the flamboyant vocabulary of Baroque.

Nicodemus Tessin the Younger, view of
the internal garden at Palazzo Tessin,
1692–1700, Stockholm

Of the Italian Baroque architects, it was Bernini who had the greatest influence on the changing styles in France, and consequently in Europe. Bernini's international reputation was such that he was even summoned to the court of King Louis XIV in France. His design for the Palais du Louvre, although unsuccessful, triggered the design of innumerable palaces all over Europe during the 17th century. During the late 17th century, foreign architects began to embark on study tours of Italy, where they worked in the building yards of the main cities. Carlo Fontana, a second-generation Roman Baroque architect, had the greatest influence on a large number of foreign architects, who were to enjoy distinguished careers in their own countries. These architects included the Swede, Nicodemus Tessin the Younger, the Austrian, Johann Lucas von Hildebrandt, the Germans, Johann Dientzenhofer and Daniel Pöppelmann, as well as the Scotsman, James Gibbs.

Austria, Germany and Poland were largely responsible for the spread of Baroque to North West Europe. By the close of the century the centrally-planned spaces of Baroque had spread as far as Vilnius (now Lithuania). Thanks to the dissemination of Baroque by Poland and the Ukraine, by the beginning of the 18th century, the new forms had even extended as far away as Moscow. However, the trend took longer to be cross-pollinated beyond Europe, starting eventually when Late Baroque was already beginning to evolve into Rococo. As with Austria and Germany, it was not until the 18th century that Spain and Portugal found their artistic expression and could thus spread the new style to their South American colonies. Generally speaking, architecture in Latin America followed Iberian and Portuguese models, without making any particularly innovative contributions. Just as Italian Baroque differed from German and Austrian Baroque, South American Baroque also contained a large number of unique local variations. Compared with the European models spread by the Jesuits (from around 1576), the various regions adopted different codes when building their great cathedrals. These codes were driven by the prevailing requirements and possibilities and were dependent on the

Salomon de Brosse, façade overlooking the Gardens of the Palais du Luxembourg, 1615–1624, Paris
The Palais du Luxembourg was originally built for the French Queen, Maria de' Medici. The exterior of the palace is reminiscent of Late Tuscan Renaissance. The Queen is said to have desired a palace modelled on the Pitti Palace in Florence, which accounts for the powerful rustication over the triple-storey façade. The employment of paired pilasters in the central section is echoed by the paired columns, thus lending gravitas to the entrance.

various artisan and building traditions of the region, thus leading to original works. Mexican Baroque cannot, therefore, be easily compared with Spanish Baroque, nor can the personal interpretations of it in Ecuador or Peru be compared. Equally, Brazilian architecture of the same period is only vaguely comparable to Portuguese architecture. The similarity between the Iberian-Portuguese models and the Central South American versions is due to the fact that both were largely based on ornamentation. *Catafalques*, *baldacchino* or 'canopies' and *camarín or* 'shrines' (all temporary or mobile structures built specifically for religious ceremonies) are typical elements of an architectural style that relied principally on decorative elements for the organisation of space. Nowhere else could European architects create such an abundance of flamboyant decoration or employ such lively and bold colours. Many of the façades echo altar structures and contain ornaments and reliefs evocative of carved wood. These embellishments are likely to have been carried out by extremely skilful local carpenters and stonemasons, and were very rare in Europe; they are a testament to the powers of survival of their indigenous artistic genres.

Metropolitan Cathedral, 1571–1813, Mexico City
The building yard at this monumental stone cathedral in Mexico City remained open for almost 250 years. The different architectural styles in the Metropolitan Cathedral seem to achieve aesthetic harmony, thanks to the continuity of local stylistic influences. The main body of the cathedral, with its simple geometry and huge dimensions, dates back to the 17th century (completed in 1667), while the façade is typically Spanish. The embellishments — ranging from real adornments to twisted columns, curved tympanum and volutes — are Baroque.

FRANCE

During the 17th century, France was one of the best suited political and social spheres for the development of Baroque — a style that offered unlimited scope for the celebration of power. The absolute monarchy of the Richelieu, Colbert and Louis XIV era, spawned an exuberant blossoming of arts and culture, driven by the desire to transform Paris into the new artistic hub of Europe. Rome, which until then had been the undisputed cultural benchmark for over five centuries, was in steady decline. Italian artists, though, continued to be summoned to the major courts of Europe. Thanks to the greater ease of international travel, the spread of Baroque was extremely swift. In a short space of time, Paris superseded Rome as the arbiter of style, whilst Colbert, who had been appointed Superintendent of the King's Buildings, decreed in 1669 that the use of curved shapes for the exteriors of buildings was inappropriate on the grounds that they were neither elegant, nor tasteful.

Thereafter a few particularly interesting spatial solutions developed, also due to the Academie de l'Architecture (founded in Paris in 1671) which established Classical reference models. The prototypes prescribed simple, stark lines, based on symmetry and balanced proportions; hence the French preference for classically elegant façades and lavish Baroque interiors during the 17th century. Rococo was to evolve just a few decades later. French Baroque urban spaces were laid out in a network where the centres were defined by the cities, which were arranged on a grid, with urban squares as the main hubs. In Paris, squares mostly contained statues of the sovereign; over the course of the 17th century, four of these squares were designed, all of them honouring the Bourbon dynasty (from Henri IV to Louis XIV). These 'royal squares' were not built according to strict pre-set plans, though they tended to be simple and easily recognisable. The earliest squares were triangular in shape (e.g. Place Dauphine, 1605), then they became square shaped (e.g. Place des Vosges, 1605–1612) finally evolving to a circular form (e.g. Place des Victoires, 1682–168 a perfectly suited backdrop for the statue of Louis XIV, the frivolous Sun King). Unlike in Italy, the squares in France were designed to be

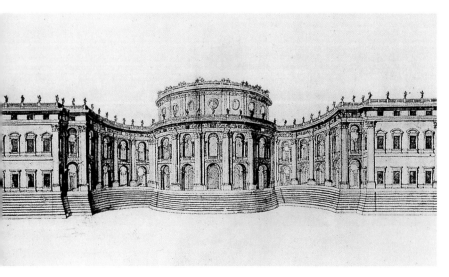

Gian Lorenzo Bernini, initial design for the front elevation of the Palais du Louvre, 1664–1665, Paris
The Palais du Louvre was destined to be the Parisian residence of Louis XIV and the Prime Minister, Colber. Leading architects of the time — Bernini first and foremost — were commissioned in the restructuring of the palace. This initial design for the façade employed the main Roman Baroque themes: dynamic, undulating lines, whilst the body of the building extended out by curving outstretched wings creating formal and visual unity. However, Bernini's design was rejected as the shapes were considered too Classical for French sensibilities. The elevation was nevertheless used as a prototype in more than one instance.

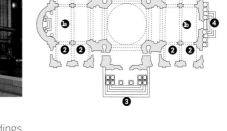

Jacques Lemercier, façade (left) and floor plan (below) for the Church of the Sorbonne, 1626–1642, Paris
The floor plan is based on an elongated Greek cross where the main axis is derived by the Classical nave (1a-1b) of an ordinary basilica onto which the side chapels are orientated (2). By placing the cupola at the intersection of these axes, Lemercier conceived a centrally-planned space that seems to extend longitudinally, thus achieving an elliptical effect. Due to the layout, both façades have the entrance (3 and 4) on their median lines, respecting the Classical symmetry so important to 17th century France. Lemercier's penchant for Classicism can also be noted in his academic approach to the composition of the façade with its stark lines deriving from the influence of Vignola and the Italian architecture of late 16th century.

straightforward urban spaces and were not tailored to the monumental buildings that defined them. The buildings surrounding the squares tended to be residences, their uniform façades arranged like a backdrop for the statue of the King, as if to emphasise the relationship between the sovereign and his subjects. Given the stable political situation in France, military defence was not an issue and, unlike cities such as Turin, there were no territorial limits to the city's expansion. The urban layout thus included wide boulevards and triumphal arches and was able to develop fluidly as an open space. It was only in France that the Baroque concept of extension into infinity could hope to be achieved, where every individual constituent part, from squares to gardens, conformed to a planned structure.

below
below
Gabriel Perelle, Place des Vosges,
1605–1612, Paris

The Place des Vosges, situated in the Marais district, was built to a square plan and is surrounded by residences for the upper echelons of society. The elevations are uniform, featuring a succession of covered arcades at ground floor level and a series of equally-sized windows on the upper levels. The only elements that create a rhythm to the composition are the dormers and the roofs, whilst the taller building contains the main entrance. This homogeneity of style and construction creates a powerful visual continuity that works in harmony with the enclosed square, which is reminiscent of a cloister. The statue of Louis XIII on horseback, erected in 1639, is situated in the centre of the square.

left
Jules Hardouin-Mansart,
view of Place Vendôme, 1686,
19th century rendering, Paris

Jules Hardouin-Mansart (1646–1708) designed Place Vendôme, as the new centre for the urban settlements that had extended beyond the city to the west. The plan of the square is an irregular octagon, created by a series of buildings that are angled obliquely at the corners. In this instance, the public space is fairly enclosed, though the north-south axial openings create a strong link between the 'exterior' and 'interior' of the square. A giant Classical column bearing a statue of Louis XIV creates the focal point on this axis. The project was intended to unify both from an urban and an architectural perspective. Thus the proprietors of the buildings on the square had to adhere to certain rules relating to porticoes, dormers, materials and heights.

THE MASTERPIECE
SAINT-LOUIS-DES-INVALIDES

The simple, stark forms of this military hospital, built by Libéral Bruant for Louis XIV, were influenced by Spanish monastic architecture at the Escorial. The complex had a long, narrow church on the central axis that originally terminated in a chapel dedicated to the sick and infirm. Mansart undertook the building of a royal, centrally-planned chapel in 1679, with a cupola, which he then built as an extension to the existing church. The accentuated vertical development recalls 17th century Italian prototypes and was the only example of its kind in French architecture during that time.

Jules Hardouin-Mansart, view of the courtyard of Saint-Louis-des-Invalides, 1670–1708, Paris
The forms of the complex respect the French Baroque desire for harmony and Classical proportions, but are also clearly influenced by Roman Baroque architecture. The majestic elevation was achieved by resting the outer cupola (built of timber and covered with lead) on an additional volume — a kind of attic with arched windows — rather than directly on the high drum.

HÔTELS PARTICULIERS

The concept of the *hôtel* — a residence for noble Parisian families — was more akin to that of a *château* or castle adapted to the urban context, than to that of an Italian patrician *palazzo*, from which it differed in both principle and typology. Grand Parisian residences tended to be articulated around wide courtyards and their distribution was such that the public rooms were at the front of the building, facing onto the street, as if to shield the intimacy of the private areas, which were only accessible by traversing the courtyards. The aristocratic Italian *palazzi* of the 17th century, on the other hand, tended to open outwards (for example the outstretched wings of Palazzo Barberini). Aside from this contrast — which also highlights the different cultural and social contexts — the other major difference between *hôtels* and *palazzi* was their physical setting. In Italian cities (with the exception of a few cities such as Naples and Genoa) there was an abundance of space and architects were able to plan spacious and elegant rooms. In Paris, however, the sites were extremely narrow and irregular and their footprint pre-established. This meant that architects had to use all their powers of ingenuity and had to plan the internal distribution, the position of the stairs and the access areas extremely carefully. The architecture had to be functional, yet grandiose. It is therefore significant that Bernini's scheme for the Palais du Louvre was rejected as being 'too uncomfortable'.

Louis Le Vau, view of the courtyard at the Hôtel Lambert, 1640–1644, Paris
The entrance to the stairway, which dominates the courtyard when entering from the street, is rendered even more dramatic by the concave surfaces and the tympanum (triangular crowning element) that frame it. A series of grand Classical columns on both levels create a majestic impression at the entrance and lead to the recessed staircase on the ground floor, thus creating an interesting play of solids and voids. As in Roman prototypes, the uniformity of the mass is assured by continuous horizontal elements (such as the tympanum) and repeated vertical elements (such as the plinths of the columns and subtely projecting piers on the lower floor).

above
Antoine Le Pautre, view towards the courtyard of the Hôtel de Beauvais, 1658–1660, Paris
The private domain is accessed through a space which is covered by a flat roof supported on convex columns leading towards the courtyard (6, see plan): the same curvature is then extended by the front wall, which presses inwards to create a perfect semicircle. A balcony supported by corbels surrounds the courtyard, providing visual and formal continuity. The lower level is rusticated, whilst the concave section has slightly regressed surfaces with large arched windows and smaller oval windows.

right
Antoine Le Pautre, first floor plan of the Hôtel de Beauvais, 1658–1660, Paris
Le Pautre managed to create an elegant courtyard (1) on an extremely irregular site, around which the building is articulated. The circulation is functional and the solution manages to exploit even the most difficult corners to the maximum. Thanks to the variety of curves, the ensemble is extremely dynamic: the only orthogonal forms are those of the spaces facing onto the street (2) which were originally designed as offices and shops and act as a filter to the private domain. At the end of an elongated lavish gallery (3) on the *piano nobile*, there is a chapel (4); below the gallery, the stables are at ground floor level and overlook both the courtyard and the garden (5).

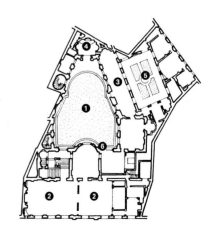

THE FRENCH GARDEN

The Court of Louis XIV (1643–1715) is generally credited with introducing the French Garden, however its origins actually derive from 16th century Italian gardens. The plan distribution along a main axis and the central position of the palace are drawn from the Italian model, beyond which everything was arranged according to a precise geometric pattern. The reason that French gardens differ so significantly from Italian gardens can be attributed to the differences in the geology of the two countries, as well as the availability of far greater expanses of space in Italy. The absence of natural inclinations and terraces helped to determine the acceptance of the concept of open space, stretching as far as the eye could see, creating an impression of infinity. The first French gardens were designed for Richelieu's castle by Jacques Lemercier in 1630. However, the popularity of gardens only reached its height after the mid-17th century. The rise of popularity was due to the landscape architecture of André Le Nôtre (1613–1700), whose schemes were imaginative, vivid and extremely structured. Le Nôtre's designs attempted to regulate all elements, nothing was left to chance and every single element was tailored to a larger overall arrangement, based on a few, simple principles. The palace formed the geometric centre of the composition and marked the journey from the city to the countryside. The transition from nature harnessed by human (flowerbeds embroidered with coloured patterns, like fine works of art), to progressively less cultivated spaces was gradual and well planned. From a visual perspective, a longitudinal axis extended from the castle to the wildest part of the garden.

Palais des Tuileries, late-18th century engraving, Paris
André Le Nôtre took charge of the rehabilitation of the Tuileries Gardens in 1667, having previously been employed along with his father (Jean Le Nôtre, gardener to Louis XIII) to tend them. Le Nôtre made substantial alterations to the 1563 scheme, which had involved a static succession of geometric forms, based on the Italian Renaissance garden. Le Nôtre introduced a primary longitudinal axis (Avenue des Champs Elysées), demarcating the direction in which the city had expanded westwards. Superimposed over the axis he layered an orderly and extremely structured system of minor axes and visual perspectives, rhythmically animated by circular fountains and squares. The intersection of these elements created spaces of varying geometric shapes.

André Le Nôtre, aerial view of the palace and gardens of the Chateau de Vaux-Le-Vicomte, 1656–1661, France
Prior to Le Nôtre's intervention, the area surrounding the chateau had been a tangled natural landscape. The site thus gave Le Nôtre the opportunity to shape the natural landscape with a totally free hand. Unlike the Italian garden, the resulting French garden creates completely open vistas, with no visual limits either to the pathways or the views, while still forming part of an overall geometric whole. Apart from the palace, all the other elements — such as the level terraces and the lakes — developed horizontally without jeopardising the principle of infinite extension. The element of water, also subdued by humans, plays a significant role with fountains and water basins bringing dynamism and vitality to the landscape, creating a play of reflections.

VERSAILLES

The Royal Palace of Versailles is regarded as the synthesis and triumph of French Baroque. The enormous building complex was commissioned and developed by Louis XIV, who adopted it as his own, private residence and that of his Court. The palace also accommodated all the administrative offices of the Kingdom of France.

The design and decoration of the palace and its gardens can be ascribed to the French artistic school, under the direction of Louis Le Vau.

In his extension of Louis XIII's hunting lodge, Le Vau respected the structure of the pre-existing complex, orientated out towards the city. Le Vau integrated the structure into the site by adding long wings; he fashioned a new frontage onto the park — although his successor, Mansart, was also involved in the conversion.

The new façade was closed in the two upper floors of the central part, where Le Vau created a large terrace. Mansart managed to create a sense of continuity in Le Vau's project. He achieved this by reintroducing the principles of French Classicism, such as the high, rusticated plinth, formal purity and symmetry. The façade is structured along twenty-five axes, animated by projecting volumes with columns that are slightly staggered.

Louis Le Vau, Jules Hardouin-Mansart, view of the façade overlooking the gardens of the Royal Palace of Versailles, 1664–1690, Versailles, France
Mansart was also responsible for adding the two long arms to Le Vau's central block, tripling the length of the façade overlooking the huge park.

**Jules Hardouin-Mansart, Hall of Mirrors,
1678–1684, Versailles, France**
When Mansart decided to enclose the
terrace that dominated Le Vau's elevation at the King's request, he built an
enormous hall with seventeen arched
windows overlooking the park. The hall
was designed to create a connection
from the King's apartments to those of
the Queen. Thanks to the splendour of
the works of art that adorned its walls,
it soon became a showcase. The interior decoration and furnishings were
entrusted to Charles Le Brun, the first
royal painter, who transformed the hall
into a jewel of French Baroque taste.
Originally known as the 'Great Hall', the
hall soon became known as the 'Hall of
Mirrors' due to the innumerable mirrors that decorate and illuminate the
interior. The silver detailing on the
furnishings was carved by the most
accomplished silversmiths of the time
and the wall hangings were exquisitely
embroidered with gold. The fresco on
the vault depicts key events in the
reign of Louis XIV, with allegories using
trompe l'œil techniques.

Jules Hardouin-Mansart, Robert de Cotte, view onto the garden of the Grand Trianon, 1687–1688, Versailles, France
Surrounded by a splendid park, the Grand Trianon was built as a more intimate residence, far from the frenzy of the Court. The complex is also known as the 'Trianon de Marbre' due to its marvellous cladding of white stone and precious marble. It is made up of several buildings, all single-storey, arranged over two wings linked by an open portico. The portico consists of paired rose-coloured marble columns supporting a linear trabeation covered with a flat roof. The horizontal development of this low, elongated complex is perfectly suited to the Baroque concept of perspectival views stretching into infinity.

left
Jules Hardouin-Mansart, Robert de Cotte, view of the altar of the Palatine Chapel, 1698–1710, Versailles, France
The Palatine Chapel is attached to the north side of the palace and is inspired by the medieval royal chapels which were arranged on two different levels. The lower floor has a nave held by arches on massive piers and was for Court use, while the upper floor was reserved for the sovereign. A luminous gallery, which correspond to the width of the side aisles, is held by powerful Classical columns. The gallery runs along the entire perimeter, linking the chapel to the King's apartment. The transparency of the volumes (with arcades and loggias) and their luminosity (assured by the numerous windows) are reminiscent of the interiors of Gothic churches, although the shapes conform to the Classical taste of the time. The refined decoration plays on the contrast between the pale stone and the blue and gold of the frescoes in the vault.

below
Pierre Patel, view of Versailles, 1668, Versailles, France
The focal point of the ideal city was the palace, whilst the Sun King's bedroom was situated at the heart of the palace, around which the entire composition was symbolically arranged. Even André Le Nôtre's (1661–1690) gardens were part of this hierarchical and geometric organisation of spaces and had to be tailored to it. The harmony between the palace and the natural context was carefully calibrated; the perspectival views always had the palace as their central departure point. Nature itself seemed somewhat artificial, as if tamed by humans to service the King; only in the Grand Park (the grounds furthest away from the palace) was nature allowed to grow more naturally, but even here everything was planned and prepared in order to facilitate hunting parties.

CENTRAL EUROPE

Catholicism was widespread in central-eastern Europe in the aftermath of the Thirty Years' War, which had caused so much suffering and persecution and had led to the 'Germanisation' of institutions.

In Bohemia, for example, Catholicism became the official State religion and spawned the development of 'Jesuit' Baroque, which employed the austere, stark forms imposed by the Roman Catholic brotherhood as its point of departure. However, it did also embrace a more elegant vocabulary thanks to Francesco Caratti, (an architect of Italian origin) and Jean-Baptiste Mathey, (an architect of French origin). Following the devastation wrought by the war in Prague, commissions from the new aristocratic class became abundant. The architects were especially commissioned to design magnificent private palaces with gardens. Italian architects tended to be in charge of the major building yards: in 1680 twenty-eight Italians were working in the city of Prague alone, (whereas there were only seven German architects). It took many decades, until the end of the century, before the numbers evened out and central Europeans took charge. This change occurred thanks, particularly, to the Dientzenhofer brothers, whose dynamic shapes influenced the various countries along the River Danube. The Jesuits travelled to Poland very early on, in 1564; where their missionary outreach was enormously successful. The priests not only built churches, but also schools in all the country's major cities. Sigmund III Vasa, the profoundly Catholic ruler of the Polish-Lithuanian Commonwealth, funded the building of several churches.

below, left
Carlo Lurago, Church of St Ignatius, 1665–1668, Prague
As was common practice all over Europe, this Jesuit church was based on Vignola's Roman model; simple, yet powerful. Trained as a stucco craftsman, Lurago embellished the upper order of the stark façade with fine stucco reliefs. The lower order is not in proportion with the elevation, the main body of which is decorated with stone statues.

below, right
Agostino Barelli, Theatinerkirche, 1664–1674, Munich, Germany
Barelli (1627–1699) was probably the leading Italian architect in Bavaria. In this church he utilised the same layout as he had done for the San Bartolomeo Confraternity Church in Bologna. The building also bears a striking resemblance to Sant'Andrea della Valle in Rome.

Before the Thirty Years' War started in 1618, the German States were undergoing a period of fervent building activity, especially related to the Reformation and Counter Reformation movements. The profound economic and social crisis that engulfed these regions only started to subside towards the close of the century. Although the 17th century could largely be regarded as a lengthy inactive spell as far as civil architecture was concerned, the same could not be said for religious architecture. A certain continuity of building work was assured by the religious orders that had left Rome to carry out missionary work throughout Central Europe. Though the buildings mostly conformed slavishly to the same prototypes and were rarely noteworthy in terms of quality or originality of design. The architects who dominated the European architectural scene for almost the entire century were secondary figures from Northern Italy, flanked by extremely skilful artisans, stucco decorators and painters. The interior designs and alterations — frequently made to the standard Roman façades — were based on local or regional characteristics and taste and are considered to be the most interesting elements of these buildings. In Austria and Germany, for example, façades were commonly endowed with two side towers covered with the typical bulb-shaped bell-towers. These buildings did, however, make a fundamental contribution to the spread of the tenets of the time and laid the groundwork for the great Late Baroque architecture that was to blossom during the 18th century. In traditionally Catholic countries, such as Austria and southern Germany, the Jesuits had been an influence since the end of the 16th century and continued to have an influence for at least a century. Meanwhile the traditionally Protestant regions (such as northern Germany), remained unaffected. Buildings inspired by the church of Il Gesù in Rome,

Jean-Baptiste Mathey, Palace of Troy, 1679–1696, Prague
This summer palace was a blend of an Italian villa with lateral wings and a French pavilion. The façade is dominated by a monumental, curved double ramp staircase, decorated with enormous allegorical sculptures. A giant order also adorns the composition of the external, simplified elevations. Despite the profusion of frescoes, the palace's most striking feature is not the interior, but rather the beautiful garden (the first Bohemian Baroque garden), which had required the hilly landscape to be levelled.

with barrel-vaulted ceilings and chapels, were erected from the Tyrol to Poland, as is made evident by buildings in numerous cities like Innsbruck, Salzburg, Coblenz, Munich, Cologne, Bonn, Krakow and Prague. The architects who were primarily responsible for spreading this particular trend include Solari, Canevale and Lurago. Italian architects who had helped to make Roman Baroque such a success in Austria flocked to Vienna, the strictly Catholic Hapsburg capital. Unlike Bohemia — where the frantic building activity began slightly later, after the defeat of the Turks in 1683 — German architects, such as Von Erlach and Von Hildebrandt in particular, only began to take over from the Italians from around 1710.

left
View of the dome and nave vaults in the Jesuit Church 1623–1631; remodelled by Andrea Pozzo, 1703–1705, Vienna
Also known as the University Church, the design was inspired by Italian churches built for the Jesuit Order. The exterior is traditionally sober, as was customary for the Jesuits, whereas the interior is decorated lavishly. The decoration was carried out in several different stages, when Andrea Pozzo was commissioned to update the interiors of the church in keeping with the latest Roman trends. The vault was therefore decorated in typically Baroque style and supported by a series of twisted columns, while the dome was painted with magnificent trompe l'œil paintings.

opposite page, top
Francesco Caratti, Cernin Palace, 1668–1679, Prague
The enormous, 144-metre-long façade is articulated by a succession of thirty-two colossal, three-quarter detached columns with decorative Corinthian capitals. This unbroken sequence of identical elements rests on a high, rusticated plinth that clearly derives from Palladian and Classical Renaissance architecture. The result is a splendid rhythmic play of light and shade; the emphatic repetition of the giant elements is a typical characteristic of the rhetorical Baroque language.

opposite page, bottom
Giovanni Battista Trevano, view of the New Palace from the canal, 1619–1625, Ujazdowski Park, Warsaw
During his reign, King Sigmund III Vasa helped to promote the architectural revival of the new capital, Warsaw (Krakow ceased to be the capital of the kingdom in 1596). Vasa commissioned leading Italian architects to build a great many royal palaces for his family. This castle was intended to be a summer residence. Trevano, the Royal Architect, designed both the palace and the surrounding park, encompassing the remains of an ancient 13th century castle. Alterations were carried out later that century to create a purely decorative canal in order to emphasise the main axis of the palace.

RUSSIAN BAROQUE

With the proclamation of the Russian Empire and the beginning of the reign of Peter the Great, the Tsar's wealthy family commissioned numerous buildings — flamboyant cathedrals in particular — creating a style that was to characterise Muscovite architecture between the 17th and 18th century. The grandeur and sumptuousness of the decorations resonated strongly with the latest European artistic vogue at that time. Consequently, the architecture produced during that period became known as 'Muscovite Baroque' or 'Naryshkin Baroque', after the Tsar's family. These buildings testify to a desire to blend traditional Russian with European Baroque elements and are particularly noteworthy for their delicate stone decorations and gilded onion-shaped domes that were influenced by Byzantine architecture. The volumes were simple and geometric; the layouts — usually on a central plan without being particularly articulated — were drawn from the Italian Renaissance. This approach was common amongst Ukrainian and Polish architects. The buildings often featured an external open gallery on the ground floor whilst the bell-towers were no longer positioned adjacent to the church but were rather to be found on the façades of the buildings, frequently directly above the central octagon, in order to accentuate the verticality of the volume.

Whereas Russian architecture was undergoing a great stylistic revolution at the close of the century, with the fusion of European Baroque and traditional elements, a complete break with the past was imminent. In the new city of St Petersburg, the so-called 'Petrine Baroque' (developed in the 18th century) stood in complete contrast to the centuries-old Byzantine tradition and cleared the way for European architects to develop the new style.

opposite page, top
Sergey Turchaninov, Church of the Resurrection in Kadashi, 1687–1695, Moscow
The five golden onion-domes make this church one of the most notable and renowned examples of Moscow Baroque. The church was commissioned by a wealthy weavers' guild; the slender red brick bell-tower was added a few years later. The contours of the surfaces and the detailed architectural elements of the bell-tower (such as the window frames and corbels, or the balusters that articulate the different levels) are constructed from white stone. The adornment reaches a visual peak with the bands crowning the elegantly carved stone stepped volumes (drums) that support the domes of the church.

Church of the Intercession at Fili, 1690–1693, Moscow
The architect of this church is unknown but was almost certainly local, as were almost all the leading Moscow Baroque architects. The elegant chromatic effect is achieved by the juxtaposition of red bricks — used for the load-bearing structure — and white stone — used for the decorative elements, columns and window frames. The volumes are arranged around an overtly vertical central space, while an external gallery runs around the base of the building, widening it and thus accentuating the pyramid effect of the architecture. The outer-most layer features a double staircase which leads to the upper floor and the entrance to the church; there is also a terrace — directly above the gallery — that surrounds the building, where processions took place.

below
New Jerusalem Convent, 17th century, Moscow
The convent was founded in 1524, however only the Cathedral of the Virgin of Smolensk — the typical onion-shaped domes can be seen to the right of the image — remains from that period. The other buildings were added during the 17th century at the behest of Peter the Great's sister. The six-storey, seventy-two-metre-high octagonal bell-tower was completed in 1690 and towers above the fortified wall. The bell-tower contains a church on the second level. The Church of the Transfiguration, dating back to 1688 (first from the left), is recognisable by its five golden domes, each surmounted by a Christian cross. The side elevations feature a pair of unusual scallop-shell gables.

ENGLAND

The situation in England differed profoundly from the rest of 17th century main-land Europe. As opposed to Italy and France where power and wealth were flaunted, England's political and social circumstances meant that it was in no posi-tion to manifest absolute power. Subsequent to the first Civil War and the 1688 Revolution, the concept of monarchy as a divine mandate faded, making it increasingly possible for oligarchic power to manifest.

This was largely due to the fact that England had been cut off from the rest of European culture for a prolonged period of time and English architecture had developed, more or less, independently from Continental Europe. The tenants of Italian Renaissance were eventually introduced to England in the early 17th cen-tury. The architect who was responsible for this was the English architect, Inigo Jones (1573–1652). It was Jones who brought the elegant œuvre of Palladio to the attention of the British. The knowledge of Palladio's work was to have a tremen-dous impact on English architecture for many years. Inigo Jones was not only an architect, but also a writer of theatrical sketches as well as a scenographer; he was appointed Superintendent of Royal Buildings in 1615. Jones' pure compositions, based on harmonious proportional ratios and clear articulation, were the antithe-sis of the prevailing Baroque taste for excess. It was not until 1660 that Protestant England began to communicate and have exchanges with its nearest European neighbours, France and The Netherlands in particular. This development sparked widespread architectural rejuvenation. Without the large commissions from Catholic Religious Orders, building activity in England was largely confined to pri-vate residences, inspired by the sumptuous French models. Representative archi-tecture looked to Versailles, whilst domestic architecture drew on contemporary Dutch housing.

Isaac de Caus, Double Cube Room, 1653, Wilton House, Wiltshire, England
The largest and most sumptuous reception room, utilised for receiving only the grandest of guests, corres-ponds to the centre of the façade. The space is a perfect cube 9.1 x 9.1 metres. The double cube, from which the room takes its name, was initially attributed to the architects Jones and Webb. The room is lavishly decorated in red and gold hues, which creates an elegant contrast to the panelled white walls. The walls are decorated with gold-leaf fruit and flower motifs. The paintings were part of Charles I's col-lection, which included a fine collection of works by the Flemish Baroque artist, Anthony van Dyck. The ceiling is pain-ted with scenes from the life of Per-seus.

Early 17th century Dutch architecture, based on Palladian symmetry and monumentality, was very simple and classical. This pared down aesthetic tied in well with the architecture of Inigo Jones. The building that most represents this typology, and which influenced both the Netherlands and England, was the noble Mauritshuis in the Hague by Jacob van Campen, built in 1633.

The architecture of 17th century England was therefore Classical in style though its forms differed enormously from those of contemporary Rome.

French Baroque was to have the greatest influence on England, whose cultural development had evolved independently from the rest of mainland Europe. There was a growing interest in Parisian architecture; Charles II (1660–1685) was evidently so inspired by the lavish projects commissioned by Louis XIV, that the Royal Hospitals in Chelsea and Greenwich were based on the Invalides in Paris, whilst Winchester and Windsor Castles were inspired by the grandiose, Palais de Versailles.

Charles II was a patron of Sir Christopher Wren (1632–1723), a brilliant anatomist and astronomer, who was later to be appointed as Royal Architect. It was, however William Talman (1650–1719) and John Vanbrugh (1664–1726), followed by Nicholas Hawksmoor (1661–1736) who built grand houses for the nobility. Their buildings are a testament to the increasing power of these landed gentry, who had risen to such an elevated level that they were able to build houses that competed with those of the King in terms of scale and luxury.

The most popular 17th century architectural typology in the immediate vicinity of London was the country house, which was often inspired by grandiose Dutch residences, albeit on a smaller scale. English aristocrats were less concerned about their London homes, unlike the French royalty, who lived in their grand Paris *Hôtels* but went to Versailles to pursue courtly life.

CHRISTOPHER WREN: CHURCHES

The 1666 great fire of London destroyed as many as eighty-seven churches, including the enormous St Paul's Cathedral. Sir Christopher Wren was elected as a member of the Royal Commission for rebuilding the scorched city and from 1670 onwards, during only a few short years he designed an astonishing number of Protestant churches (over fifty, mostly small-scale). Wren's designs tended to be based on a rectangular plan, a simplified basilica model, sometimes without side aisles. Wren's designs were novel; he managed to harness the opportunity in order to test his ideas and, in some instances, came up with extremely interesting solutions that took Baroque principles of harmony and spatial dynamism to great heights. The formal aspects of his designs, on the other hand, were not inspired by 16th century Roman buildings and remained true to the Classical Palladian aesthetics that Inigo Jones had introduced into England. Wren devoted a great deal of attention to the bell-towers and spires of his churches, turning them into unique creative features that were interesting from both a formal and an urban perspective. His (unrealised) master plan for London's urban renewal was reminiscent of Roman and Parisian solutions, with squares and radial streets converging at a central point (in this case, the Stock Exchange). Peripheral roads had religious buildings as their focal points. Wren's spires were designed as landmarks as well as embellishments for the urban landscape. These new perspectival nodes, therefore had to be highly visible and identifiable.

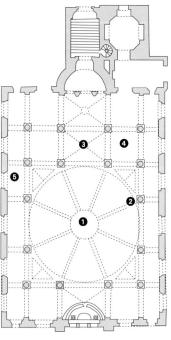

Engraving and plan of St Stephen's Walbrook Church, 1672–1677, London
At first glance, the floor plan of St Stephen's looks extremely simple, however, its linearity is in fact based on a complex combination of central and longitudinal axes. A massively oversized dome (1), relative to the small size of the church, is placed over a rectangle, giving the impression that this is the central space, whereas the plan shows that the building is actually a longitudinal, basilica-type space. The dome is held by twelve small columns (2), which form a square and support a network of criss-crossing arches; as well as the eight arches (3) that connect the columns to the central octagon (beneath the dome). There are minor arches (4), which connect the octagon to the square that create triangular shapes on the plan.

THE MASTERPIECE
ST PAUL'S CATHEDRAL

St Paul's was the first English Protestant cathedral to be built after the 14th century split from the Catholic Church. The cathedral was designed to symbolise an official architectural style representation of the Anglican religion. The volumes and lines of the church are clearly drawn from St Peter's. The scale and majesty of the cathedral testify to the desire to trump Rome architecturally; the rivalry is implicit in the monumentality of the building. The dome had no formal precedent in England. Wren's passion for geometry is clearly evident in the formal purity, the proportions and the symmetry of the imposing building – all clearly influenced by Renaissance architecture.

Christopher Wren, Saint Paul's Cathedral, 1675–1710, London
The overall impression of the façade is undeniably Classical, yet it nevertheless contains elements that are Baroque: the eccentric-looking lantern, the paired columns in the centre and especially the ground floor windows which were designed to look like alcoves, thus playing perspectival tricks typical of Baroque. These oddities aside, the tension and dynamism that characterise typical 17th century Roman façades are lacking and, although the dome is extremely high, the upward thrust is weak and its typically Renaissance proportions are somewhat static.

THE MASTERPIECE
THE ROYAL HOSPITAL

Both the Chelsea Hospital and the Royal Naval hospital — for soldiers and sailors respectively — were built by Wren for Charles II. The structure of the Royal Naval Hospital, although a great deal more grandiose, was clearly inspired by Chelsea. The hospital is a unique architectural complex; its monumental shapes and forms create a prominent focal point on London's urban landscape.

top
Christopher Wren, interior of the Painted Hall, Royal Naval Hospital, 1696–1704, Greenwich, England
This enormous painted hall — hence its name — in the Naval Hospital was conceived by Wren as the dining room for retired sailors at the Royal Naval Hospital in Greenwich. The hall was decorated by James Thornhill (1708–1727) with various trompe l'œil images and an enormous oval painting on the ceiling. It forms part of a building that also contains a domed atrium and a further hall on the upper floor. Large arches on different levels link the various spaces.

bottom
Christopher Wren, Royal Naval Hospital, 1696–1704, Greenwich, England
This magnificent perspectival axis starts on the banks of the Thames and runs through the entire Royal Naval Hospital complex, terminating at Inigo Jones's Queen's House. Wren mirrored the buildings along this longitudinal axis embellishing them with theatrical elements, such as the long porticoes with paired columns and the slender twin domes that unify the composition and add solemnity to the succession of spaces.

THE MASTERPIECE
CHATSWORTH HOUSE

This magnificent country house was commissioned by the first Duke of Chatsworth. The position of the palatial house in the rural landscape is superb; overlooking the River Derwent with the wooded hills as a backdrop. The building was adapted to accommodate the incline of the site, which accounts for the fact that the elevations have different numbers of floors. The western and northern elevations were probably built by Thomas Archer. The front façade features an imposing central entablature supported by columns, which underscore the symmetry of the composition. The park is regarded as the first great English Baroque garden and contains hills, follies, sculptures, fountains and artificial lakes.

Thomas Archer, view of the West Front of Chatsworth, 1700–1703, Derbyshire, England

William Talman, view of the South Front of Chatsworth, 1687–1696, Derbyshire, England

SPAIN

Spain reached its apogee under Philip II (1556–1598); it was during his reign that masterpieces such as the Escorial in Madrid were built. By the close of the 16th century and the reigns of Philip III (1598–1621) and Philip IV (1621–1665), Imperial power was shaken by a crisis of enormous proportions. This was a time of deep public discontent, revolts and political corruption, not to mention the Thirty Years' War and general economic decline. Hopes of architecture flourishing in any way, let alone in a style representing absolute power, were dashed. The development of Baroque was largely only in terms of superficial decoration, at times taken to extremes and used for rhetorical purposes, to astonish the population and distract them from reality. The Spanish passion for adornment was rooted in 15th and 16th century architectural tradition, when the intricate decorative Plateresque style took over from the typical Moorish and Gothic style of decoration. Churriguerism then took over during the second half of the 17th century; this was an even more flamboyant and overstated genre of ornamentation, which took its name from the Spanish sculptor/architect, José Benito de Churriguera, who was largely active in Salamanca. This sumptuous style reached its height during the 18th century, especially in the South American colonies where the rhetorical language of Baroque art was truly exploited. The decorations created an unspoken, pictorial language, which could easily be understood by the local population, even it they were illiterate.

below, left
Jerez de la Frontera, façade of the Charterhouse of Santa Maria de la Defensión, 1667, Cadiz, Spain
The stately façade looks rather like a stone altarpiece consisting of three superimposed elements that contain a geometric arrangement of niches with sculptural reliefs. The pyramidal layout of the tripartite division underscores the central axial symmetry of the composition. The lowest tier rests on a base heavily decorated with floral motifs and escutcheons and has pairs of Ionic columns framing superimposed statues; the middle tier is similar to the bottom one, but rather than a curved entablature, it has a broken one, which almost seems to open up in order to make room for the third element which bears a sculpture in the centre. The entire façade is covered with an excess of, at times, somewhat unruly decoration: a large number of decorative vases are crowded onto the upper part of the middle tier.

below, right
Alonso Cano, view of the western front of the Cathedral, 1664–1667, Granada, Spain
The linear forms of this building, which to some extent mark the beginning of Spanish Baroque, are still heavily drawn from 16th century Renaissance. Cano was a painter and sculptor as well as an architect; his multiple talents informed his design of the façade, which he treated as if it were a sculpture. Cano's façade thus has great plasticity — it is subdivided by three enormous arches, extended over two levels, one of which is common to all three arches whilst the second only features on the individual elements. The play of projected and recessed, niche-like sections, creates deep shadows and enhances the dramatic effect.

Diego Martínez Ponce de Urrana, Royal Chapel of Nuestra Señora de los Desamparados, 1652–1667, Valencia, Spain
At the termination of the longitudinal axis, vis à vis the entrance (1, on plan) there is a camarín (5, on plan), which is a space above the altar for displaying the sacrament. The interior decoration is extremely sombre, whilst the space communicates a sacred, spiritual atmosphere. The manner in which the entire composition has been structured, (i.e. the interconnection of the various spatial elements that lose their individual autonomy to become part of a single central organic space), is however undoubtedly Baroque.

right
Diego Martínez Ponce de Urrana, plan of Nuestra Señora de los Desamparados, 1652–1667, Valencia, Spain
This is a centrally-planned church which consists of an oval inscribed in a square; it is developed along a longitudinal axis that runs perpendicular to the front façade. The composition is perfectly symmetrical. Besides the main entrance (1), there are two additional subsidiary entrances on each side elevation (2) that connect to the central space through the wide openings in the inner walls (3). These openings are also arranged symmetrically, as are the chapels on the transversal axis (4).

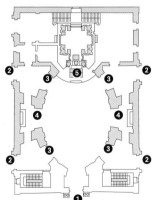

left
Church of Nuestra Señora del Pilar,
1681–1754, Saragoza, Spain
The church is a place of pilgrimage;
built around an alabaster column
where the Virgin Mary is said to have
appeared. The original plan layout is
Baroque and was designed by Royal
Architect, Francesco de Herrera the
Younger, subsequently the project was
continued by Felipe Sánchez. This
enormous building is one of the largest
Spanish Baroque religious buildings.
It is characterised by a large dome
and a series of smaller domes, with
four angular towers demarcating each
corner. During the 18th century further
extensions were added by Ventura
Rodriguez.

bottom, left
Detail of the roof of the church of
Nuestra Señora del Pilar, 1681–1754,
Saragoza, Spain
The eleven domes are clad with colou-
red tiles arranged in geometrical pat-
terns, which date back to the 18th cen-
tury.

opposite page, top
Juan Gómez de Mora, Pedro Matos, view
of the façade of the Cathedral and the
Jesuit church of the Clerecía, 1617,
Salamanca, Spain
The influence of 16th century Spanish
architecture can still be detected in the
symmetrical articulation of this façade
and the simplicity of its forms. The
elements are arranged according to
a strict gridlike geometric pattern of
vertical lines (columns) and horizontal
lines (string course cornices) that sub-
divide the façade into sections where
the windows are situated.
The linear geometric scheme is adorned with a wealth of decoration, rather
unusual for the Spanish Renaissance,
which indicates the transition towards
Baroque.

bottom
Juan Gómez de la Mora, Plaza Mayor,
1617–1619, Madrid

Plaza Mayor is unique and should therefore not be regarded as being a representative example of 17th century Spanish Baroque, but rather as an early and unique town planning exercise. The enclosed public space was modelled on the early Parisian royal squares, suitable for hosting public festivals. The rectangular plan layout is surrounded by triple-storey residences with repetitive façades and a continuous arcade at ground level.
The linear, continuity of these elevations is enlivened by nine access entry doors and two centrally-placed buildings that face each other across the longer axis: the Baker's House to the north and the Butcher's House to the south, distinguished by two lateral towers. A statue of Philip III was placed in the centre of the square as a focal point.

PORTUGAL

It was largely due to the religious reasons that Baroque architecture never really took hold in Portugal. The 16th century Protestant Reformation had not taken root in Portugal and therefore, lacking the rivalry, Catholic religious orders did not have to make an overt effort to spread their word. When Portugal reasserted its independence from Spanish domination in 1640, it chose to embrace an architecture that reflected its nationhood almost as if to preserve its own identity, rather than embracing the new Baroque style. The forms of buildings were simple and stark and evocative of military and monastic architecture. This similarity was so marked that 17th century Portuguese Mannerism, devoid of ornamentation, was compared with 16th century Spanish architecture. Religious buildings in Portugal tended to be simple basilica spaces with twin bell-towers on the façade. Churches were extremely practical and functional and were unadorned both on the interior and on the exterior. The architecture consisted of volumes based on Classical proportions and on clear geometry. The simple construction enabled this prototype to be repeated throughout the Portuguese Empire. Baroque was eventually introduced to Portugal during the late 17th century, possibly as a result of Guarini's design for Santa Maria della Divina Provvidenza in Lisbon. However, the new spatial and formal Baroque elements were not greeted with great enthusiasm; thus truly Baroque buildings in Portugal were few and far between. Ironically, rather like with Spain, the best Portuguese architecture was not produced there, but in its Brazilian colonies during the 18th century.

below, left
The Palacio Fronteira Gallery of Arts, 1640, Benfica, Lisbon
The terrace leading to the chapel unfolds like an open-air gallery, its walls characterised by a succession of twelve arched niches covered with gigantic panels decorated with *azulejos* (ornamental tin-glazed ceramic tiles), alternating with smaller niches containing statues. The statues were designed to be personifications of the Arts and mythological figures.

opposite page, right
Baltasar Alvares, façade of S Lourenço or Grilos (Our Lady of the Crickets) (Church and convent of S Lourenço), 1622, Oporto, Portugal
The monumental grey stone façade exemplifies the Portuguese national style of architecture. Drawn from Mannerism, this style was in vogue until the late 17th century. The façade is conspicuous for its simplicity of form and the absence of any embellishment. The curious name of the church, 'Our Lady of Crickets', derives from the Augustinian friars who took ownership of the, initially Jesuit, building complex.

View of the exterior and gardens of Palacio Fronteira, 1640, Benfica, Lisbon
Portugal did not begin to recover from its economic crisis until 1640, when the aristocracy started building magnificent residential palaces. The first Marquis of Fronteira turned a simple hunting lodge into this huge complex in Benfica, where there is a palace followed by an incredible flow of landscaped gardens (five and a half hectares in size). Though modelled on 16th century villas with Italian gardens, the dynamic articulation of the elements that create the circulation paths and vistas, reveals a Baroque influence.

Nature has been tamed and used to create outdoor architecture: the hedges were trimmed into topiaries symbolizing the seasons; there are also a great many fountains and water basins as well as flights of stairs and grottoes. The most fascinating features are undoubtedly the use of varied ceramic tiles and shells as ornamentation.

FROM BAROQUE TO ROCOCO

During the 18th century, architecture consisted of a combination of different contemporary styles. By the late 17th century, Baroque vocabulary had reached its peak in Italy — the country where it had first developed — and had subsequently been adopted throughout Europe, where it had evolved naturally and in a variety of ways depending on the specific context and the specific architect. The era of absolute powers and ecclesiastical hegemony — characterised by a celebratory and magniloquent aesthetic — gradually gave way to the new century, which was marked by sweeping political and social change. Although the reign of Louis XIV had come to an end in 1715, his example apropos visionary building projects was to prove a long-lasting model for many of Europe's sovereigns, who looked to the Royal Palace of Versailles not just as the *non plus ultra* of centralised power, but also as a piece of exquisite architecture and a model of prestige and magnificence that was revisited by numerous Late Baroque designers.

Architects and artists developed a stylistic code based on magniloquence and monumentality in order to underscore and communicate typical Absolutist values, such as the glory and authority of the sovereign as a divine right. This encompassed the Late Baroque style, an offshoot of the multi-faceted evolution of 17th century aesthetic/architectural development in Europe during the first half of the 18th century.

One of the underlying principles of Late Baroque art was the concept of *synthesis*: a synthesis of forms, stylistic traits and aesthetic qualities. The desire to combine different traditions was not merely confined to relationships between the artistic disciplines, but also to the blending of different artistic styles. Buildings had to be able to improve upon previous models: for example the phenomenal Roman and French sources of inspiration, as exemplified by San Lorenzo in Turin and Versailles outside Paris.

Johann Bernhard Fischer von Erlach,
view of the cupola of the Karlskirche,
1715–1737, Vienna

The varied social, political situations and artistic traditions in each European country produced an infinite variety of expressions and interpretations. In Italy, Roman Baroque was on the wane, while capital cities like Turin and Naples reprised the vocabulary of Baroque, producing extraordinarily inventive versions of Rococo. Rococo was a style that had evolved in France during the early decades of the century and flourished alongside Late Baroque. The movement embraced an entirely different approach, casting magniloquence and monumentality aside in favour of hedonistic flights of fancy where fantasy, prettiness, frivolity, sophistication and pleasure were valued. As the new century dawned, people were eager for freedom and cosmopolitanism, relaxation and distraction. *Douceur de vivre* or the 'sweetness of life' was taking over from the *grande manière* 'grand manner' and Baroque splendour was being ousted in favour of Rococo gaiety. This development was principally expressed through interior decoration where precious materials were used along with muted, pastel colours, mirror effects, exotic ceramics, stuccoes and rare woods crafted with extraordinary mastery. The interiors of palaces altered and were subdivided into numerous drawing rooms, parlours and intimate boudoirs that replaced the excessively large and flamboyant 17th century spaces. The changing pastimes and habits of the aristocracy had a direct impact on architecture that lead to the design of smaller rooms of even greater originality and sophistication. The new trend advanced quickly to the other European countries. The element of fantasy promoted the inventive creativity of architects, particularly in Central Europe. The rise and consolidation of powers such as the Austrian Hapsburg Empire after its victory over Turkey and Frederick II's Prussia, triggered a lengthy series of public and private commissions that were to change the face of many Central and Eastern European cities. In short, 18th century Late Baroque differed from 17th century Roman Baroque primarily due to its ethereal elegance, the luminosity and spaciousness of the interiors, the reduced scale and the minute attention to detail and interior decoration.

Baroque architecture, and Late Baroque architecture in particular, tended to break the rigorous Classical codes. A rational, balanced approach, based on harmonic proportions and geometric rules gave way to a new, far less constrained approach: celebratory, decorative, fantastical and enthralling. The spectacular fusion of architecture and decoration, typical of Rococo, took Baroque architecture on a completely different tangent towards an independence and freedom that would have been inconceivable during the late 17th century. The stylistic exuberance of Late Baroque, often regarded as excessive, but actually manifesting an

François de Cuvilliés, external view of the Amalienburg Pavilion in Nymphenburg Park, 1734–1739, Munich, Germany
This pavilion reveals the influence of French Rococo on German architecture. It is modelled on the Petit Trianon Château at Versailles, with a main circular room, known as the Hall of Mirrors and two wings with ample fenestration. The pavilion was built as a hunting lodge within the grounds of Nymphenburg Park, which was the summer residence of the Bavarian kings.

Nikolaus Pacassi, Great Gallery at the Castle of Schönbrunn, begun 1744, Vienna
The Great Gallery belongs to the great extension scheme for the castle, situated outside Vienna. The gallery was commissioned by the Empress, Maria Teresa of Hapsburg, and was inspired by the French Hall of Mirrors in Versailles. Pacassi designed the front façade overlooking the garden, as well as the chapel, Court theatre and the alterations to the internal spaces, which were white and embellished with gilded stuccoes. The frescoes on the vault were painted in 1760 by Gregorio Guglielmi and depict the Allegories of War, Arts and Sciences as well as the Austrian provinces.

extraordinary ability to break free from rules and preconceptions, thereby shrugging off the rigidity of the Classical model that was deemed to be the undisputed height of architectural perfection. Architects were increasingly emancipated, not just due to their technical skills (they were often experts in engineering and mathematics), but also thanks to the contagious enthusiasm that the patrons had for Baroque extravagance. Using the architecture as a medium, patrons vied with one another to try to arouse the greatest astonishment and wonder: eccentricity and prestige, opulence and power were combined in a heady mix. The boundaries of architecture were pushed; moving from the physical realm into the realm of illusion, with the help of painting and sculpture. Numerous bold structural experiments were undertaken, where the borders between what was possible and what was impossible appeared to vanish. The domes and wide ceilings of churches and palaces were notable for their disconcerting powers of optical illusion, opening out into bold perspectives, more powerfully expressive and emotive than ever before. This architecture of illusion was not solely focused on decoration; rather it sought to visually increase the scale of a space that might otherwise have seemed constricted. Thus, for instance, the claustrophobic effect of excessively low or heavy ceilings could be counterbalanced using illusion. The effects increased, so that the boundaries of real architecture and painted or sculpted architecture could no longer be distinguished from a certain, well-calibrated distance. This ability played a major role in the visual drama of Late Baroque.

Sacred Buildings

The most significant manifestations of Late Baroque architecture are to be found in Central Europe, where the schism between the Reformation and the Counter Reformation was more marked and architecture assumed a new, proselytizing role on a vast territorial scale. Religious buildings were supposed to move the soul and inspire the intellect in an era where the mysteries of faith were to be supported. European Catholicism spread the idea of monumental 'monastery-courts' with important monasteries, such as those at Melk on the Danube (1702–1738) and Ottobeuren in Germany (1748–1766), as well as votive churches such as the Basilica of Superga (1715) near Turin. These complexes served as 'beacons' on the landscape; milestones of faith. Sacred buildings, commissioned by kings, princes, bishops and abbots were erected in the same spirit as the royal palaces of Caserta, Stupinigi, Würzburg and Vienna. Sacred architecture emphasised the

new spatial complexity of Baroque even further, adding vigour, lightness and spaciousness to the soaring volumes. The undulating rhythms first introduced by Borromini and the compelling concave-convex effects of Guarini became real *tours de force* during the 18th century, with their curved plastic articulation, bursting with energy. Late Baroque architecture explored the fusion of longitudinal and central plans, creating 'centralised longitudinal' churches and 'centrally-planned elongated' churches with an open, flexible spatial design. Architects were genuinely fascinated by central plans, however the longitudinal axis remained a vital component in designs for the great missionary churches and monasteries.

With his litany of pulsating and interpenetrating elements, Guarini became the inspiration for the great European architects. Masterpieces such as the German Benedictine church in Banz by Johann Dientzenhofer (1710–1713) and the Vierzehnheilingen Sanctuary by Balthasar Neumann (begun 1743) were the result of a calibrated, precise and intellectual approach, comparable to the contemporary *contrapunto* musical compositions of Johann Sebastian Bach. Furthermore, light played a fundamental role in sacred buildings, as a unifying and uplifting element in the spatial continuum of Italian-inspired Baroque. Examples of this are the Chapel of Sant' Uberto (1716) by Filippo Juvarra at the Royal Palace of Venaria — where light confers a slightly profane atmosphere, reminiscent of a theatre — and Bernardo Vittone's church of Santa Chiara in Bra (1742) — with its pierced vaults, cupola and pendentives, which allow light to permeate throughout the space.

The evolution of the 18th century Catholic Church, with its penchant for great centralised domed spaces and spatial units illuminated with light, created churches similar to those of a typical Protestant church. Thus, George Bähr's Frauenkirche in Dresden (1726) is a transparent, centrally-planned structure, where the primary space is surrounded by a complex system of 'light chambers'.

Dominikus Zimmermann, interior of the Pilgrimage Church of Wies, begun 1743, Germany
The architect arranged the oval layout of the church over unusual quadrangular paired piers and inserted a deep choir in order to emphasise the perspectival effect. The sumptuous rocaille stucco decoration diverts the eye from the structure of the building: the white and gold stuccoes are the epitome of Bavarian sacred architecture, creating an indissoluble entirety.

Behind the typically 'Borrominian' convex façades, the interiors are embellished with a rhythmic, syncopated series of interpenetrating oval spatial cells: the effect is heightened by three-dimensional arches. Thus architecture and decoration are rendered inseparable. This fusion was to take place in southern Germany to a greater extend than elsewhere. In Bavaria, most Rococo architects were also great artisans, like the stucco artisans of the Wessobrunner School, as well as the Asam brothers, who built the church of St Johann Nepomuk in Munich, (1746–1750) and Dominikus Zimmermann, who built the Steinhausen Pilgrimage Church and the Sanctuary of Wies (1744–1754). The pale stucco and gold interiors seem to constantly change as the light reflects off them, thus becoming real *Gesamtkunstwerk*, i.e. unified works where all artistic disciplines are united by a flood of light, awash with whites, golds, pinks and pale blue hues.

The same vital exuberance can also be found in Southern Europe. In Spain and Portugal, there was particular attention paid to the importance of surfaces, inherited from Islamic and Plateresque art. This can be discerned in the wall planes adorned with *azulejos*, the proliferation of relief tracery and the exaggerated theatrical effects, as in Narciso Tomé's *Transparente* (1721–1732) in Toledo Cathedral. In Sicily, the fantastical façades with their convex central, towering sections (e.g. at Noto, Ragusa and Modica), articulated in exuberant bands of piers and half columns, were early examples of the harmonious formal and functional combination of the façade and bell-tower.

Urban Spaces: Squares and Large-Scale Public Buildings

Symmetry, centrality and axiality were elements used to communicate the influence and control of the dominant power. These elements also recur in new urban plans and road systems: from Rome to Prague, from Paris to Turin, all the way to St Petersburg. Rationally organised space became the focal point in the conception of cities. In the context of Late Baroque urbanism, the architecture of city squares was infused with a particular symbolic role. City squares became a fundamental constituent of the urban hub and formed a backdrop to community life. Squares enjoyed particular popularity in France during the 18th century as *places royales*, surrounded not by public buildings, as in Italy, but rather by identical private residences built for the bourgeoisie.

These elegant squares, which framed the monuments to the sovereigns that were the central focal points (such as Place des Vosges in Paris, 1605–1612), were used as prototypes to be replicated in cities all over Europe right up to the

18th century. The squares were mostly situated directly in the centre of the cities, or else in close proximity to the royal residences. They were largely grandiose places, used to host lavish festivals and parades. Their symbolic meaning, however went beyond being a mere homage to the sovereign, to become part of a more complex plan where urbanism and politics merged. *Places royales* were frequently built, not only in a celebratory vein as backdrops to equestrian statues of the king, but also to flaunt wealth. Squares were local interventions and required functional restructuring, becoming the cities' commercial and administrative focal points. Many capital cities were forced to extend or restructure ancient town plans whilst squares served as fulcrums for new urban plans. Urban development still rested firmly in the hands of the monarchies. From a stylistic point of view, the monumental Classicism of urban squares was often uplifted by elegant Rococo overtones. Inspired by 17th century French squares, monumental spaces were built in various European locations, such as the octagonal Amanlienborg Square in Copenhagen. In 1749, Frederick V commissioned the Danish architect, Nicolaj Eigtved, to build one of the most beautiful urban squares of the entire 17th century; where the centrality of absolute monarchy and the flamboyance of Rococo were perfectly combined. The creation of a true *place royale* to the north of Copenhagen's ancient city centre — with four palaces arranged diagonally around an octagon — was the focal point of an enormous restructuring programme in the Frederiksstaden district. The square was endowed with a clear point of reference: in the huge domed church on the side of the square's shorter axis. Another important square was Place Stanislas in Nancy (former Place Royale, 1751–1755), named after the Polish King, Stanislaos Leszczyski, who became Duke of Lorraine in 1737 and who intended to dedicate the square to Louis XV. The architect, Emmanuel Héré, surrounded the square with a series of elegant aristocratic residences whilst one of the sides featured a grand access gate to the park. In Bordeaux, France, Jacques-Ange Gabriel built an enormous square (Place de la

Eugénio dos Santos, Commerce Square, begun 1758, Lisbon
During the mid-18th century, Lisbon was one of the largest and most densely populated cities in Europe. In 1755, a devastating earthquake, followed by an enormous tsunami, destroyed a large part of the city. The Prime Minister, the Marquis of Pombal, decided to rebuild the city according to a new city plan. He decided to create a huge square where the ruined Ribeira Royal Palace once stood: Praça do Comércio, or Commerce Square, situated next to the River Tago, near the port, remains one of the largest squares in Europe. An unvaried series of public buildings, linked to trade and port activities, was erected around its perimeter. The Portuguese architect, Eugénio dos Santos, designed a rational plan for the large U-shaped square, which is open to the river on one side and terminates with two towers. Several alterations were made to the scheme. A bronze equestrian statue of King José I was erected in the centre of the square. The sculpture was executed by the leading sculptor of the time, Joaquim Machado de Castro.

Bourse, 1749) with the imposing Palais de la Bourse situated on the northern side, surmounted by an equestrian statue of Louis XIV. The elegant and classical lines of the building make it one of the finest examples of 18th century Late Baroque.

The increasing number of small and large cities can be ascribed to the intensely urbanised culture of the 18th century and the changing face of Europe. The form of the cities, their town planning solutions and the architecture of the buildings, were all very efficient and incisive vehicles for imprinting the new political and social scenario onto the image of the city.

In capitals all over Europe during the 18th century, royal palaces were transforming into complex, multi-functional administrative centres. Rational, innovative architectural solutions were developed for secretariats, offices, archives, libraries, art collections as well as for theatres, the latter opening its doors to a large public. The creation of new building typologies was a social phenomenon, driven by the cultural climate and new ideas. Streets, squares, public and private buildings, water features, innovative furnishings and landscaped gardens all combined to imbue the urban plans with meaning. By the close of the 17th century, many of the medieval charitable institutions for the destitute and infirm, previously run by religious orders, were passed into the hands of state administrators who altered their structure and function. The 'benevolent government' and the consequent centralisation and control of every aspect of civil life spawned large, new functional buildings: namely, hospitals. The San Gallicano hospital in Trastevere was built during the 1720s by the Italian architect, Filippo Raguzzini. Although he largely adhered to the traditional Roman hospital plan layout, with linked wards, he also came up with innovative functional and hygienic solutions, creating a new concept for the public health service. In 1742, Ferdinando Fuga was commissioned to extend the capital's oldest hospital, Santo Spirito in Sassia. The interior was subdivided into a series of spaces, according to function and capacity, such as the new anatomical theatre — symbol of modern medicine — devoted to discovering treatments for diseases

rather than simply accepting them stoically. New public offices were set up in France for managing the hospitals. These institutions sheltered paupers and the sick, thus removing a large number of beggars and vagabonds from the city streets. Behind the ethical motivations there also lay a desire to free the cities from an increasingly large marginalised social class. The Hôtel-Dieu in Paris, founded in the 9th century, was extended in order to give a permanent home to hundreds of poverty-stricken people. The refurbishment and extension of the Hôtel-Dieu in Lyons was entrusted to Jacques-Germain Soufflot (1713–1780) in 1741.

The new urban plans and the modernised, efficient facilities devised by Europe's progressive governors around the mid-18th century, sparked the plans for the huge poorhouse, Real Albergo dei Poveri, in the Kingdom of Naples, conceived by Fuga in 1748. The architect employed an austere 16th century vocabulary in order to emphasise the stern perspectival effect of the volumes; the thoroughfares and the functions of the powerful complex all radiated out from the central church. The Albergo was, however, to remain an incomplete monument to the (unrealistic) aspiration towards order and centralisation that had spawned similar buildings elsewhere in Italy to house the underclass (e. g. Ospizio in Genoa, San Michele in Rome, as well as others in Palermo, Venice, Modena and Turin).

The Domestic Space: A Desire for Comfort

All through the 18th century, the residences of the wealthy classes underwent enormous change, thanks to the triumphant rise of the bourgeoisie who, despite their new-found wealth and their consequent aristocratic ways of life, embraced values and habits that involved a relatively more moderate lifestyle. This new state of affairs began in France: with the death of the Sun King in 1715, many noblemen and women left Versailles and returned to Paris. This prompted the refurbishment and renewal of their palaces or the construction of new homes in keeping with the new architectural trends of reduced spaces and successions of smaller rooms rather than the grand, sumptuous 17th century *appartements*. A sense of practicality and elegant sophistication prevailed. Aesthetic beauty was sought on

Ferdinando Fuga, Real Albergo dei Poveri, begun 1748, Naples
Fuga designed a vast complex that was to accommodate approximately 8.000 impoverished people and beggars, who would otherwise have had to fend for themselves, often through crime. The Real Albergo dei Poveri had to be able to accommodate as many as 1.000 rooms, five great courtyards as well as an immense six-aisled church. Only a section of the mammoth construction was constructed; the façade facing the street is an incredible 600 metres long, even larger than the Royal Palace at Caserta. The scheme is harmoniously Classical, arranged on five floors, with a monumental double flight of steps demarcating the main entrance.

a smaller scale and functionality became important, while design lost none of its sophistication. Boudoirs — private parlours where women received their most intimate guests — began to be in vogue. These were charming, smaller-scale spaces that were ideally suited to more intimate and private interactions. These rooms were also easier to heat during the winter months.

In Paris, which had become the benchmark for Europe as a whole, there was a proliferation of the so-called *hôtels particuliers*, elegant town houses with sober, classical façades that masked their elegant interiors. Entrance courtyards (*cours d'entrée*), flanked by various utility areas such as stables or kitchens, led to the residences proper, generally arranged on two levels and thus screened from the exterior. There were usually delightful private gardens behind the houses. The streets containing these *hôtels particuliers* became fashionable, such as those in the Marais district, especially the area around the 17th century, Place Royale (later Place des Vosges), and the Faubourg Saint-Honoré.

The Hôtel de Matignon (1722–1725), the Hôtel Amelot de Gournay and the Hôtel de Soubise (1704–1709), were considered to be among the finest Rococo town houses in Paris.

Architecture and interior decoration were affected by the significant social changes that took place during the 18th century, such as the swift ascendency of the bourgeoisie, the stark reduction of aristocratic and clerical power, as well as the spread of Illuminist and scientific ideas. Thus the triumphalism of absolute power, monarchy and Church was lost in the face of a changing social and cultural trend towards hedonistic delight and pleasure. The fascination with the sumptuous Royal Palace of Versailles soon waned after the death of the Sun King in 1715; however the rest of Europe took longer to change course. Although the triumph of reason and practicality might have brought a re-dimensioning of spaces, in no way did this remotely signify a move towards aesthetic or decorative sobriety. Rococo architecture was quintessentially elaborate; its gilded stuccoes, lacquers, mirrors and its light structures — where the play of colours served to emphasise the luminosity and spaciousness of the interiors — the imaginative juxtaposition of spaces, such as oval or circular parlours alongside more traditional rooms, with an

Jacques-Germain Soufflot, Hôtel-Dieu, begun 1741, Lyons, France
Soufflot built the imposing white stone Classical façade along the Rhone. The main entrance has a wealth of decoration adorning it. The elegant cupola, erected during the second half of the century, was intended to improve the flow of air around the great communal rooms below. The Hôtel-Dieu was continued by Soufflot's pupils, and became one of the largest buildings in Lyons, sheltering and tending to the vastly increased numbers of poor people after the lengthy period of conflict that had battered France. On the strength of this project, Soufflot was summoned to Paris, where he built the Pantheon.

almost labyrinthine quality, were all aspects that created new heights of flamboyance. Rococo decoration was based on abstraction and asymmetry; the forms were derived from nature such as shells, corals, flowers and *racemes*, not to mention the passion for the exotic — *chinoiserie* in particular. The structural elements of buildings — previously powerfully accentuated — disappeared completely behind the optical trickery and illusions of the décor. For the first time architecture and decoration were fused as one inseparable element. The intellectual magniloquence of Baroque gave way to gaiety, sophistication and purely sensory pleasure. Architecture was now governed by interior decoration.

opposite page, left
François de Cuvilliés, Hall of Mirrors, 1734–1739, Amalienburg, Munich

opposite page, right
Real Fabbrica di Capodimonte, porcelain cabinet at Palazzo di Portici, 1757–1759, Capodimonte Museum, Naples

opposite page, bottom
Place de la Bourse, 1730–1755, Bordeaux
Part of the bastions of Bordeaux were demolished in order to make way for the Place de la Bourse on the west bank of the Garonne, with two lodge-style buildings situated opposite one another: one is the Palais de la Bourse (north side) and the other is the Hôtel des Fermes, which is decorated with sculptures of Minerva and Mercury.

Jean Courtonne, courtyard façade of the Hôtel de Matignon, 1722–1725, Paris

THEATRES

Theatres were one of the increasingly popular types of building throughout Europe during the first half of the 18th century. By the beginning of the century, the Baroque theatre had fully developed in Italy and the prototype was imitated in many Northern European countries.

Late 17th century Baroque theatrical architecture introduced structural alterations that were to become universally accepted. Stage sets became more realistic and were staggered to give an illusion of depth, the traditional tiers and open galleries were abolished and replaced with auditoriums containing rows of boxes divided by columns and arches, bestowing greater intimacy and comfort. A few examples of these typically Baroque theatres include: Ferdinando Galli Bibiena's Teatro Ducale in Mantua (1706) and the Teatro Filarmonico in Verona (1729) designed by Francesco Galli Bibiena. The theatre boxes were projected to slightly different degrees with slightly different forms: bell-shaped or horseshoe-shaped, to improve the view of the stage. Not all architects adopted this solution, however. In France, for example, the auditoriums tended to be rectangular.

There was a major difference between private Court theatres and public theatres, which were not to develop fully until the late 18th century. Generally speaking, both kinds of theatres were built to a similar kind of plan; varying in scale and character. Court theatres were an integral part of palace buildings and did not, therefore, need a specific architecturally-defined aesthetic to display to the outside world.

François de Cuvilliés, Residenztheater, 1751–1753, Munich, Germany
The Residenztheater was Cuvilliés final masterpiece; one of the most flamboyant Rococo theatres in Europe, lavishly decorated in gold and ivory, with stucco caryatids and sculpted musical instruments. The layout and structure are traditional, while the ornamentation includes undulating horizontal walls, tortile columns and beautifully sculpted telamons.

On the other hand, public theatres were urban spaces and were, externally at least, self-contained pieces of architecture.

From an artistic and architectural point of view, one of the most interesting and valuable Late Baroque theatres to have survived is the Residenztheater in the Royal Palace in Munich; a true Rococo gem. In 1750, Maximilian III Joseph, Elector of Bavaria, commissioned the French architect, François de Cuvilliés, to build a new theatrical opera house in collaboration with scenographer, Gianni Paolo Gaspari.

The theatre opened three years later, in October 1753. The extraordinary, almost entirely timber interior, is embellished with marble balusters and columns, friezes, stucco, *cartouches* and *intaglio* with splendid gilding, according to the typical tenants of Rococo. The grand royal box for the sovereign and his family is truly sumptuous, taking up two rows of smaller boxes. The box is crowned with the family crest and swathed in elegant Rococo adornment.

The vault was covered with frescoes by Johann Baptist Zimmermann, featuring mythological figures. The extensive use of timber enhanced the acoustics of the

Giuseppe and Carlo Galli Bibiena, interior view of the Court Theatre, 1744–1748, Bayreuth, Germany
Giuseppe and Carlo Galli Bibiena's Court Theatre is a typical example of a mid-18th century theatre, with U-shaped rows of boxes and a proscenium framed by an arch. The Margrave's box, embellished with elaborate decoration, is strategically placed for the optimal view of the perspectival backdrops.

theatre tremendously. The Opernhaus in Beyruth (1744–1748), built by the architect-scenographer, Giuseppe Galli Bibiena, for the Margrave Frederick of Brandenburg-Bayreuth is considered to be one of the finest Late Baroque theatres in all Europe. Galli Bibiena used a combination of Italian and French elements: rows of galleries enclosed by elaborate balusters and timber boxes with decorated fronts on either side of the dominating royal box, which formed the focal point of the auditorium. A pair of columns demarcates the stage within the auditorium space. Antonio Galli Bibiena, Giuseppe's brother, reprised the idea of proscenium boxes in the Teatro Scientifico dell'Accademia in Mantua (1767–1769), the last great example of Late Baroque theatre. Erected where an earlier, small theatre had once stood, the new theatre had four orders of proscenium boxes arranged in a bell-shape.

Inside, the theatre is finely decorated with balusters, columns and stylish brackets. Vanvitelli's small Court Theatre at the Royal Palace of Caserta belongs to the same Late Baroque period. The theatre is round and embellished with twelve elegant columns. The five circular rows of boxes contain forty-two boxes in all, which are decorated with masks, stuccoes and festoons. Stage sets during the first half of the 18th century were complex architectural creations built by *quadraturisti*, artists specialised in designing perspectival and illusionistic architecture.

Quadratura, like architectural trompe l'œil, provided an opportunity to create spaces as if out of nowhere; extending rooms and multiplying them, in a dramatic

Antonio Galli Bibiena, Teatro Scientifico, 1767–1769, Mantua, Italy
The Teatro Scientifico in Mantua owes its name to the fact that it was formerly used by the Institute's School of Science and Literature, which was housed in the same building. The theatre's layout is bell-shaped, with four tiers of boxes and a fixed stage; the monochrome Arcadian panels on the sides of the boxes were also executed by the architect, Antonio Galli Bibiena.

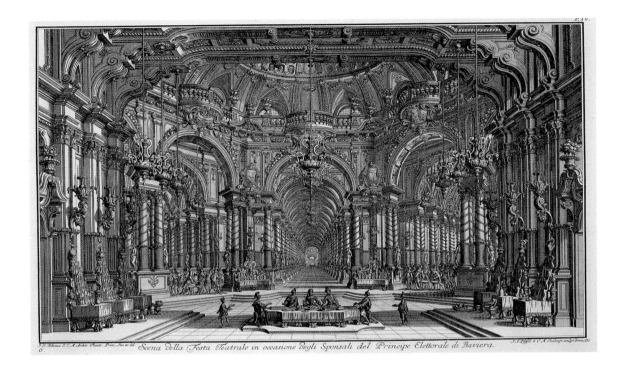

Scena della Festa Teatrale in occasione degli Sponsali del Principe Elettorale di Baviera.

play of illusions. The Late Baroque passion for variety, multi-directional and visually deceptive spaces sparked the development of this artistic movement, not just
in theatres, but also in private residences and churches. The Galli da Bibiena family of artists and architects (who adopted the name of their home town in Reggio
Emilia) developed to its heights between the late 17th and the early 18th century.
The designers excelled in painted stage sets and perspectives, executing brilliant
works all over Europe, creating architectural projects and stage sets that deceived
the eye and provided illusionistic visions of rooms and stages. The Galli Bibbiena
family were prominent due to the sophistication, imaginative and exuberant quality of their work; containing highly complex staircases, colonnades and gigantic
atriums opening out onto marvellous, animated landscapes. Ferdinando Galli Bibiena (1657–1743) invented the *scena d'angolo* (meaning 'sets at an angle'), which
provides an oblique perspective rather than the traditional centrally axial view.
This animated the box area, enlarging it and breaking up its monotonous centrality. Antonio Galli Bibiena (1697–1774), Ferdinando's son, also achieved international success as a theatrical engineer in Vienna and as a manufacturer of theatrical stands for festivals and celebrations. In around 1745 Antonio oversaw the
restructuring of the Court Theatre in Vienna, built by his uncle Francesco; on his
return to Italy, he worked as a scenographer as well as an architect, building Teatro
Scientifico dell'Accademia in Mantua, (1767–1769) and the Teatro dei Quattro Cav-
alieri in Pavia.

**Giuseppe Galli Bibiena, *The Theatrical
Celebration in Honour of the Nuptials of
the Bavarian Elector*, from Architecture
and Perspectives, 1740, Augusta,
Germany**
Foreshortened, theatrical colonnades
and balusters, vaults open to the skies,
majestic staircases and deep galleries
enhance the illusion of greater and
more magnificent interiors. The painting is inspired by classic, lofty Renaissance architecture.

LIBRARIES

The fashion for collecting artefacts and books from the late 16th century onwards, meant that libraries and *Wunderkammern* — rooms in which collectors kept their collections of objects that were special in terms of intrinsic qualities and appearance — were very much in demand. The trend for displaying precious artefacts, natural objects and handmade tools alongside one another, culminated in the Late Baroque libraries, where the discoveries of science were juxtaposed with rare natural samples. These snug libraries/studies, similar to the 'chambers of wonders,' were still common throughout the 18th century. Frederick II's library in the Sanssouci Palace in Potsdam is the best example of its type — a small, private space arranged along the lines of a Humanist study. Alongside these, the monumental libraries of the most powerful Courts were built, generally consisting of large, high rooms, lavishly frescoed, with walls covered with books all the way up to the ceiling. The libraries frequently had side rooms where curious, exotic objects were preserved. The Hapsburg Library, designed by Fischer von Erlach for example, is held in a majestic room, lit by huge windows and decorated with frescoes by Daniel Gran that allegorically depict Emperor Charles VI as the protector of arts and sciences. These libraries were not confined to princes and emperors, however: following a centuries-old tradition of knowledge conservation, monastic libraries embraced the Late Baroque flamboyant exuberance typical of their secular counterparts.

below, left
Library at Melk Abbey, 1720–1736, Melk, Austria
The Melk Library is an astonishing example of Late Baroque interiors, with inlaid, gilded bookshelves and ceiling covered with frescoes by Paul Troger, depicting an allegory of Faith overseeing earthly knowledge.

below, right
Library at the Jesuit Clementinum College, 1721–1727, Prague
Jorge Luis Borges mentions the library, a symbol of the old city of Prague in one of his books thus: "God is in one of the letters of one of the pages of one of the four hundred thousand books of Clementinum."

bottom, left
Johann Bernhard Fischer von Erlach, Hofbibliothek, 1721–1735, Vienna
While the exterior vocabulary is authentically French Classical, the interior of Fischer von Erlach's *Hofbibliothek* or Court Library, features a grand, oval domed chamber from which the arms of two imposing galleries with paired columns extend. The chamber is brimming with energy; adorned with extremely fine materials, making it one of the most fascinating interiors of its period.

top
Library at Metten Abbey, 1722–1729, Metten, Germany
The frescoed vault and stucco decoration by Franz Josef Holzinger and the precious inlaid and gilded bookshelves create an extremely emotive atmosphere. The library is one of the finest examples of European Late Baroque.

EXOTICISM

The 18th century passion for Oriental decor turned into a vogue, which was expressed in several different avenues: from *chinoiserie* to Indian patterning, from Islamic decoration to Japanese art. Faraway, exotic China, with its delicate art, was the greatest catalyst of this new trend that permeated every sphere, from interiors to architecture, decoration to porcelain, furniture to jewellery and from carpets to fine fabrics.

Graceful and elegant Rococo was a perfect medium for these exotic influences with their delicate, stylised Oriental motifs, the antithesis of rigid Classical and Baroque examples. Architects and decorators embraced the delicate *chinoiserie*, casting aside the dictates of Classical art and turning to nature for inspiration. Western architects saw the Orient as an escape route from traditional Classical schemes, enabling them give full reign to their imaginations, unfettered by codified principles.

There was a superficial trend for the exotic, rather than a genuine academic interest in Oriental art and architecture; thus original Oriental features were formally and decoratively re-examined. China started to produce objects and decorative pieces destined specifically for the European market, such as porcelain dinner services and pieces of furniture.

France and England were the countries most gripped by this frivolous and exotic trend. Aristocratic houses were crammed full with precious china, silks and large painted fans, as well as lacquered furniture, decorated fabric and timber screens. Curious pagoda-like pavilions, based on the 17th century porcelain Trianon at Versailles were mounted in gardens.

London became a flourishing market, not just for imported goods, but also for excellent imitations — especially lacquered furniture and trinkets — produced by skilled artisans and marketed all over Europe.

opposite page, top
Carl Fredrik Adelcrantz, Chinese Pavilion, 1763, Drottningholm, Sweden
The Chinese Pavilion (Kina Slott) in the garden of the Royal Palace of Drottningholm, near Stockholm, was commissioned by King Adolf Frederik in 1753, as a birthday gift for Queen Louisa-Ulrica. In 1763, the timber Chinese Pavilion was replaced by a brick pavilion, built by Court Architect, Carl Fredrik Adelcrantz, which has been preserved to this day. Both the exterior and the interior are excellent examples of the European reinterpretation of Chinese art. The artists could freely indulge their fantasies and create a fairytale, a bizarre or exotic world; though it had to resonate well with Rococo. The Queen was absolutely astonished when she discovered the pavilion, which she could use as her own personal refuge, transporting her, as if by magic, into the ancient Oriental Empire.

left and opposite page, bottom
Johann Gottfried Büring, detail and external view of the Chinese Tea House in Sanssouci Park, 1754–1757, Potsdam, Germany
The tea pavilion, built by the architect, Johann Gottfried Büring, is symptomatic of the curiosity about the Orient and passion for *chinoiseries* at that time. Built at the suggestion of Frederick the Great, the tea house is a perfect blend of nature and architecture, where gilded palm-shaped columns, imaginary full-size gilded Chinese figures (by Johann Gottlieb Heymüller and Johann Peter Benkert) holding musical instruments and cups of tea, all serve to emphasise the exotic atmosphere.

ROCOCO IN ITALY

During the 17th century, the vocabulary of Baroque first spread from Rome throughout Europe, making Rome an obligatory stopover for architects and artists who were interested in learning new approaches. During the first half of the 18th century, the great architectural foment of the previous century began to subside and architecture began increasingly to be based on tried-and-tested, rather than innovative, solutions. Some cities became sites of great urban transformation, such as, for instance, the destroyed port of Ripetta on the Tiber, built by Alessandro Specchi (1688–1729) in 1705. The port featured a double flight of stairs alongside a curved flight of stairs that connected to the riverbank.

Works by architects such as Specchi, Raguzzini, Sardi and Valvassori, all enlivened the magniloquent 17th century language into a sort of Baroquette, more frivolous and more decorative, with some Rococo elements. For years, however, the Accademia di San Luca had been calling for a return to Classical architecture and the rejection of Baroque excess. Architects such as Alessandro Galilei and Ferdinando Fuga, who executed elegant and calibrated Classical works, also supported the rejection of Baroque tenants.

Alessandro Galilei, façade of San
Giovanni in Laterano, 1732–1737, Rome

Alessandro Galilei (1691–1737), Court Architect to the Grand-Duke of Tuscany, won the competition for reworking the façade of San Giovanni in Laterano in 1732. His elevation was strictly orthogonal, relying on a giant order of pilasters that unified the superimposed porticoes of the entrance and the Loggia of Blessings. The other great talent from Clement XII's building yard was the great Florentine architect, Ferdinando Fuga, whose ability to design buildings with sobriety and elegance was ideally suited to the commission requested for the new Pontifical Rome, as exemplified by the façade of Santa Maria Maggiore (1741–1742).

Florentine born, Ferdinando Fuga (1699–1781) was extremely adept at combining Classical and Baroque styles, creating beautiful, dramatic designs. Fuga decided to keep the not-quite-dormant Classical trend alive, strenuously supported by both the Accademia and by Pope Clement XII, who was also Tuscan born. Fuga executed his most important works in Rome, which was the artistic and architectural capital during the 17th century. These works included the imposing Palazzo della Consulta (1732–1737), which had a harmoniously calibrated and formally refined façade and the façade of the Basilica di Santa Maria Maggiore (1741–1743), for which Fuga designed a double entrance loggia, the upper one of which was used by the Pontiff for his 'urbi et orbi' ('to the City of Rome and to the World') benediction. Fuga was appointed Papal Architect by Pope Clement, thus receiving several major commissions. One of these commissions included the completion of the Palazzo del Quirinale, to which he added another wing, known to locals as the 'long sleeve'. Fuga's alterations to Palazzo Corsini (1732–1736) were notable in terms of Late Baroque; here his sophisticated, elegant style radiates. Fuga was also responsible for the churches of Santa Maria dell'Orazione e Morte (1733–1737) and for Sant'Apollinare.

Fuga moved to Naples as Court Architect to Charles III of Bourbon in 1751, where he received prestigious commissions such as the building of the Albergo dei Poveri (c. 1750), several aristocratic residences, the restructuring of the royal apartments, the restoration of the Court Theatre, as well as the façade of the Church of the Gerolamini (1780). His later works showed a lack of his earlier creative freedom in favour of a more sober and Classical approach. Fuga also designed and built Villa Favorita (1768) and Villa Jaci at Resina; he also worked on the restructuring of the interior of Palermo Cathedral (1767).

It would be impossible to pigeonhole the artistic genius, Giovan Battista Piranesi (1720–1778), whose work was complex and varied. Piranesi's work is generally

top
Ferdinando Fuga, façade of Santa Maria Maggiore, 1741–1743, Rome
Fuga matured in the flamboyant Baroque tradition, which he attempted to rationalise in this sober, measured façade adornment. His Roman projects are evidence of his move from designs that were rooted in Baroque spatiality to original forms tending towards a new interpretation of Classicism.

categorised somewhere between Neoclassical and Romantic; as the precursor of both movements. However, chronologically speaking, he lived directly in the middle of the Late Baroque era and was a contemporary of architects like Fuga, Galileo and Vanvitelli. Although Piranesi was a fervent admirer of Ancient Roman art and architecture, his vistas, his use of diagonals and his methods and techniques made him more of a Late Baroque master. Unfortunately none of his built projects survive; his atmospheric engravings did however survive to illustrate his innovative architectural inventions that testify to a new Antiquity, filtered through the visionary and expansive precepts of Baroque. Piranesi was an architect first and foremost, he even signed his engravings 'Venetian architect'. His *vedute* 'views' of both Ancient and modern monuments are essentially architectural reproductions, with few figures, sketched in a similar manner to Francesco Guardi. There were many variations of Late Baroque but they all aspired to be monumental, over-scaled buildings, aspects which were echoed in the scale of Piranesi's engravings. He tended to fill the entire piece of paper with his drawings and use the largest sized sheet he could find. It is no coincidence, therefore that some of Piranesi's *vedute* depicting great Roman arches, bridges, masonry thermal vaults, often inspired painters who had fervently embraced Baroque, such as Jean-Honoré Fragonard and Hubert Robert. The visionary, universally acclaimed Carceri Complex (1745–1761), is often cited as the harbinger of Romanticism and sublime architecture, deriving from Late Baroque, phantasmagorical opera sets. Piranese seems to have known these scenographies intimately, as is evident from the myriads of drawings and engravings of works by Ferdinando and Francesco Bibiena, which feature foreshortened views of buildings with theatrical, solemn, atmospheric atriums and gloomy prisons hung with bolts and pulleys, with staircases that descend into the murky depths. Piranesi's etchings elucidate the theatrical nature of Late Baroque, a typical characteristic of the works of the greatest architectural engraver of all time.

Filippo Juvarra, interior view of the Chapel of Sant'Uberto, 1716–1730, Venaria Reale, Turin
The Greek cross plan has a longitudinal dynamic due to the filter of the entrance atrium and the repositioning of the apsidal wall, set back and preceded by a semicircular colonnade. The effect is heightened by the altar, a circular aedicule on two circles composed of six columns. Behind the altar, the muted light illuminates a great oval framed by stucco angels and clouds. The piers terminate in four small circular *tempietti* carved out of deep alcoves, behind elegant balusters, where the Court took part in services, bathed in light radiating from the cupola.

ROME: SCENOGRAPHIC CITY ARCHITECTURE

During the 18th century, Rome acquired a considerable number of ostentatious buildings, executed in order to complete or improve unresolved, neglected parts of the city. Late Baroque architects not only designed new churches and palaces, but also urban spaces, such as the famous cascading Spanish Steps at Trinità dei Monti (1723–1726) intended to connect the 16th century church of the same name, on the crest of a hill, with the Piazza di Spagna below. The original plan was designed by Francesco De Sanctis (1693–1740) and was clearly drawn from the architecture of both Bernini and Specchi: the dividing ramp, convex and concave and the semicircular terrace at the top of the steps are clearly derived from Specchi's scheme for the Port of Ripetta. De Sanctis' version was, however more complex and structured, due to the considerable distance between the church of Trinità dei Monti and the Piazza di Spagna. The imposing, noble double-flight stairway has pleasant terraces and there are benches that run all the way to the top, to create a brilliant combination of practicality and Baroque monumental aesthetic. De Sanctis drew up the project with both far and near vistas in mind, so that the various scenic views of the imposing staircase changed and multiplied as one approached along the Tiber to the Piazza di Spagna. Piazza Sant'Ignazio (1727–1730), designed by the Neapolitan architect, Filippo Raguzzini (1680–1771), is another example of a theatrical urban space. Raguzzini followed Pope Benedict XIII Orsini to Rome, and was responsible for laying out the square in front of the 17th century church of the same name. The architect lined the front of the square with apartments for the bourgeoisie, their animated, curved façades creating an ideal frame for the central oval flanked by two smaller ovals, an inspired solution that conferred dynamism and greater depth. Unlike the gracious monumentality of the Spanish Steps, Raguzzini's design created a more intimate smaller-scale public space, set against a backdrop of palaces with understated façades. The square is an enclosed urban space, typical of Rococo style — one stumbles upon it almost by chance as it nestles among the folds of the dense urban fabric;

Filippo Raguzzini, view of Piazza Sant'Ignazio, begun 1727, Rome
Buildings that had formerly stood in front of the church of Sant'Ignazio were demolished in order to make way for new buildings that the Jesuits could use to generate funds. When designing the square on the site available to him, Raguzzini entered into the Jesuits' mindset, imagining a theatrical scene unfolding outside the church, with three, new split-level buildings acting as the backdrop.

THE MASTERPIECE
THE TREVI FOUNTAIN

The Trevi Fountain is arguably one of Rome's most theatrical monuments. The fountain, hidden within the dense urban fabric, was built by the architect Nicola Salvi (1697–1751) who won a competition organised by Pope Clement XII Corsini in 1732. The Pope wanted to give a definitive appearance to the water basin at the end of the only remaining functioning Ancient Roman aqueduct. Since Antiquity, a *nymphaeum* (ancient monument to springs) had served to hold the cascading waters. The fountain is set against one of the shorter elevations of the magnificent Palazzo Poli, where Pope Urban VII had commissioned Bernini to design a monumental fountain in the 17th century. The fountain was begun in 1732, but only completed thirty years later by Giuseppe Pannini.

Salvi designed a monumental water basin with a tall, flamboyant travertine marble cliff animated by groups of sculptures, set against a solemn, Palladian architectural backdrop that is reminiscent of the ancient triumphal arches built by the Roman emperors.

A statue of Neptune, God of the Seas, in the great central niche, stands upright on a shell drawn by winged seahorses, alongside a frightened horse, calmed by a Triton.

The Trevi Fountain (probably so named because it stands at the junction of three roads — *tre vie* — is a magnificent example of a typical Baroque fountain, i.e. a work of art that perfectly blends architecture, sculpture and natural elements, in this case stone and water), like a wondrous stage animated by unusual and marvellous elements. The main theme is the sea, symbol of the progression of time, change and movement. It is precisely this concept of movement that inspired the design of the fountain: the irregular rocks, the endless flow of water animating the large water basin and the splendid figures held in eloquent poses and powerful torsions.

Nicola Salvi, Front of the Trevi Fountain
1732–1762, Rome

TURIN: A EUROPEAN CAPITAL

It was thanks to Vittorio Amedeo II di Savoia, who became King of Sicily in 1713 and King of Sardinia in 1720, that Piedmont managed to acquire widespread power and prestige, thus fulfilling its ambition of breaking free from the influence of France and its expansionist aims. The capital of the new kingdom aspired to become a significant European city in keeping with the times: a symbol of a strong and steadily ascending monarchy. The city and surrounding territory had already undergone substantial transformation during the final decades of the 17th century, with a labour-intensive programme of Baroque aristocratic residences. Vittorio Amedeo II was the driving force behind the renewal, commissioning Filippo Juvarra (1678–1736), the first Court Architect as from 1714, to modernise the city, providing not just new urban spaces but also improved, up-to-date infrastructure. The experience that Juvarra had gathered with Carlo Fontana in Rome served him well; he learned the different architectural codes from his masters, from Ancient monumental to Renaissance and Baroque codes, thus acquiring great versatility. Each of Juvarra's designs was imbued with a particular stylistic variation depending on the location and function of the building concerned. Juvarra was requested by the King to undertake a massive urban rehabilitation programme which would uplift Turin and make people admire it as a modern European capital. Juvarra built religious buildings, most importantly the imposing Basilica di Superga (1717–1731) and the princely palaces. He also planned urban spaces, such as the military barracks near Porta Susa (1716). These elegant new Late Baroque schemes transformed the face of Turin, changing it into a grand and modern city. The renewal project was so successful that it became a prototype for other cities. Juvarra surrounded himself with a skilled workforce, establishing a team that worked continuously and systematically. Furthermore, Juvarra also worked on the new fittings and furnishings for the Palazzo Reale, the hub of Savoy power and administration.

below, left
Filippo Juvarra and Benedetto Alfieri, Gallery Beaumont, 1733–1766, Palazzo Reale, Turin
When Juvarra travelled to Madrid in 1735, he was followed by Benedetto Alfieri, in his capacity as first Court Architect. They decorated the second level of the royal palace and renovated a few splendid spaces including the Gallery Beaumont (previously the Galleria della Regina and today the royal weaponry arsenal). The refined play of surfaces, the plasterwork of Pietro Giuseppe Muttoni as well as the ceiling fresco of Claudio Francesco Beaumont depicting the story of Aeneas, are portrayed with great ease and finesse.

below, right
Pietro Piffetti and Francesco Ladatte, two-piece article of furniture, 1732, Palazzo Reale, Turin
This unusual piece of furniture was produced by the cabinetmaker, Piffetti, in collaboration with the sculptor, Ladatte, who made the bronze figures. Both parts are imbued with the elegant lines typical of the 18th century.

**Filippo Juvarra, view of the interior
of San Filippo Neri, 1715–1730, Turin**
The construction of San Filippo Neri
church was begun during the late 17th
century. The drum and cupola that col-
lapsed in 1714, were rebuilt by Juvarra
according to an entirely new design. In
terms of plan layout and scale, the
church appears to be a reformulation
of Leon Battista Alberti's longitudinal
basilica plan, as in the mid-15th century, Sant'Andrea in Mantua. Like the
Basilica Superga, the church was a
'Juvarrian' ensemble of centrally-planned churches. The high, spacious vault
is bathed with light that comes flood-
ing in through the wide oval windows
that correspond to the side chapels
and is enhanced by more light that illuminates from the upper level. Juvarra
employed the concave piers and vaults
that terminate the church at both ends
to emphasise the spatial unity of the
nave and chapels: an example of the
nonchalant manner in which space was
manipulated during the 18th century to
achieve an overall effect.

Javurra's lavish, yet measured architecture, translated the great courtly fervour of
that era into a cohesive aesthetic language. The leading craftsmen of the time —
painters, decorators, silversmiths and cabinet-makers — were all summoned to
the Court to make a contribution to the new capital city.

By the time he was in his early thirties, Juvarra's extraordinary abilities and
grandiose ideas had already been recognised and his talent was sought-after
throughout Europe by kings, princes, cardinals and aristocrats. He was renowned
for his swift, accurate drawings: his designed every single architectural, decorative
and furnishing detail with instantly comprehensible broad perspectival and pictorial drawings. He recommended the artisans for carrying out the interior decoration and obsessively oversaw the painters he had selected to carry out the work.
The projects that established Juvarra as one of the leading 18th century European
architects were largely carried out during his tenure as Royal Architect during the
reign of Vittorio Amedeo II of Savoy, from 1714 onwards. Juvarra excelled at rein-
terpreting the architectural codes of his predecessors in the light of the kingdom's
new urban requirements, carrying out a major series of interventions, reinventing
the symbolic form of the city of Turin and enveloping the surrounding territory in
an all-powerful new language. During his twenty-year tenure in Turin, Juvarra built
or renovated sixteen palaces, eight churches, more than twenty-four altars, two
imposing city gates, as well as the Basilica di Superga, the hunting lodge at
Stupinigi and Venaria Reale. The sheer amount of work he managed to produce,
without ever losing sight of innovation or compromising his rigorous standards,
was truly incredible. His renovation of Piazza Castello and Palazzo Madama set the
tone for his renewal of Turin, conceived on a scale and attention to detail to rival
any of the more recent and grand European Courts. Juvarra's work on residences
beyond the city was just as incisive: his designs ceased to be mere '*corone di*

delizie' (crowning glories) but rather became projections of power, as seen from the rectilinear, monumental and civic roads that linked the buildings to the Palazzo Reale, the symbolic centre of the Savoy capital. The walls of Palazzo Madama are testament to the 2.000 year history of the city of Turin, from its foundation by the Romans to the first Senate of the Savoy reign (1848). Sitting on the former site of the great ancient gate, the building was originally the East Gate of the city, but was changed into a fortress with corner towers and sturdy walls during the Middle Ages. The name refers to the two '*madame reali*' (women regents) who lived in the palazzo during the 17th century: the first was Cristine Marie of France, who ruled the dukedom on behalf of her son, Charles Emmanuel II as from 1636, and the second, Maria Giovanna Battista di Savoia-Nemours, Charles Emmanuel's widow, who ruled it on behalf of her own son, Vittorio Amedeo II from 1675 for five years, until 1680.

The imposing frontage of the building, consisting of the current façade with a giant order, atrium and double staircase, is also the work of Filippo Juvarra, who worked on it from 1718 to 1721. Although his original grand design never reached completion (two wings were to be recessed, intended to link the Palazzo Madama with the Palazzo Reale), the façade and staircase are testament to Juvarra's sensitivity in grafting a Baroque façade onto an existing medieval building. The sombre façade has enormous French windows, alternating with piers surmounted by an entablature and a sophisticated, elegant baluster bearing vases and sculptures. The interior, which is bathed in light, is dominated by the monumental Grand Staircase that leads to the first floor, embellished with stucco garlands and shells. The stairway terminates on a spacious landing that acts as a roof for the entrance below. The palazzo was transformed into an elegant noble dwelling, a suitable symbol for representing the lineage and ascent to power of the rulers. In 1848, the enormous drawing room on the *piano nobile* was to be the seat of the first Subalpine Senate.

Filippo Juvarra, façade of Palazzo Madama, 1718–1721, Turin
Juvarra created the giant order on the forepart of the façade in a bid to achieve permeable continuity between the exterior and the interior of the building. The architect was able to incorporate the existing medieval structure on the axis of the ancient entry gate crossing the city, leading to the road towards Susa and France. A high baluster runs along the cornice, embellished with life-size allegorical statues and vases by Giovanni Baratta.

THE MASTERPIECE
THE BASILICA DI SUPERGA

The Basilica di Superga (1716–1731) is situated on a hill overlooking the city of Turin. The church is considered by many to be Filippo Juvarra's greatest masterpiece. Juvarra was the Court Architect who changed the face of the city.

The basilica is the most imposing Late Baroque sanctuary in Italy. It was built to fulfil a pledge to place a statue of the Virgin Mary on top of the Superga hill, during the time that Duke Vittorio Amadeo II of Savoy's French troops laid siege to Turin in 1706.

Juvarra reduced the height of the hill by about forty metres, devoting himself particularly zealously to this project, assiduously overseeing every single construction stage (he even wanted to be buried there, a request that could not be fulfilled as he died in Madrid). Basilica di Superga was inaugurated with a solemn mass in 1731, in the presence of King Charles Emmanuel III and Juvarra himself.

A crypt in the shape of a Latin cross was built under the presbytery to house the remains of sixty members of the House of Savoy in the 1770s.

Filippo Juvarra, view of the exterior of cupola of the Basilica di Superga, 1716–1731, Turin
The exterior of the basilica, which was designed with meticulous attention to the proportions of its volumes, is reminiscent of the Roman models of the Pantheon, which created the foundation for the development of the octagonal plan surmounted by a circular drum and cupola. It also echoes the façade of St Peter's. The pronaos, with its eight Corinthian columns, surmounted by an entablature, is visually harmonious. The cupola is flanked by two elegant bell-towers.

NAPLES

During the 18th century, the southern Italian city of Naples was characterised by the relatively short Hapsburg period (1707–1734) and the subsequent creation of the Bourbon Kingdom. A great many new building yards were established under Charles III (1734–1759) and his son Ferdinand IV (1759–1799), which changed the face of the city, enhanced with palaces, squares and new arterial roads. During the earlier Austrian Viceroyship, architects such as Domenico Antonio Vaccaro and the aristocrat Ferdinando Sanfelice, had distinguished themselves with their designs for elegant Late Baroque churches and palaces. Examples of these projects include: Palazzo Tarsia, the churches of San Michele Arcangelo and La Concezione at Montecalvario by Vaccaro; Palazzo dello Spagnolo with its famous double-flight staircase, as well as Palazzo Sanfelice and Palazzo Serra di Cassano di Sanfelice. After the Bourbons rose to power, many projects were built at their behest, such as the Royal Palace, the Albergo dei Poveri, the aqueduct and the Teatro San Carlo, built by Giovanni Antonio Medrano in 1737. Attracted by a more austere style of Classicism, Charles of Bourbon summoned the architects Luigi Vanvitelli and Ferdinando Fuga to the Court around the middle of the century. Their work — a combination of Late Baroque brio and austere Classical magniloquence — brought about a perceptible change in architectural taste locally.

Fuga devoted himself to the enormous unfinished project for the Alberto dei Poveri, the façade of which is over 300 metres long, and later, from 1778 onwards, to the famous Granili alongside the Ponte della Maddalena (demolished after the Second World War).

Luigi Vanvitelli became one of the leading Neapolitan architects during the 18th century and was commissioned to build the magnificent Royal Palace of Caserta — the 'Versailles' of the Kingdom of Two Sicilies. He was also responsible for other major works, such as the Foro Carolino (now Piazza Dante), the church of La Missione ai Vergini, as well as the restructuring of the Basilica della Santissima Annunziata Maggiore.

opposite page
Domenico Antonio Vaccaro, interior of the cupola of the church of La Santissima Concezione, Montecalvario, 1718–1724, Naples
La Santissima Concezione is considered as Vaccaro's masterpiece: the architecture, sculptures and paintings were all produced by him. The church is built to an octagonal plan interpenetrated by a Greek cross. The architect accentuated the light-coloured areas with stucco drapery placed at salient points and cartouches with sculptural figures in the pendentives. Vaccaro did away with the drum and the structural components of the cupola, so that it looked like a kind of tracery descending from above.

Domenico Antonio Vaccaro, Chiostro di Santa Chiara, 1739–1742, Naples
Vaccaro's sensitivity radiates from his most famous work. In this monastery, reality and fiction are blurred in the continuous play of colours inside the majolica-tiled cloister. Vines were painted onto the piers that support a pergola and there are images of fish painted on the bottom of the fountains.

THE ROYAL PALACE OF CASERTA

In 1751, Charles de Bourbon entrusted Luigi Vanvitelli (1700–1773) with designing a new royal residence at Caserta, where he also wanted an efficient and rational complex of barracks, administrative offices and venues for art and culture. Modelled on the most famous 17th century royal residence, the Palais de Versailles, Charles de Bourbon decided to build an imposing palace, not far from Naples, that would reflect his political prestige. In fact it was only the Royal Palace and the park that were ever realised: work slowed down in 1759 after the King of Spain's departure to head the Spanish throne and was completed by Carlo Vanvitelli, son of Luigi Vanvitelli. The architect was a proponent of an architectural code based on Classical tenants and balanced harmony; he thus designed an orderly system of buildings around the Royal Palace. A long, elegant French-style garden was laid out along a perspective axis beyond the palace complex. The enormous oval square in front of the palace, surrounded by a number of buildings, is connected to a majestic avenue that faces Naples. The access roads and palaces are linear and symmetrical, with excessively long, neat façades. The architectural scheme, as an entirety, is based on the principle of symmetrical regularity and rhythm with regard to both the buildings as well as the huge garden. The residence consists of an enormous rectangular block inside which the cruciform block of buildings configures three equal, symmetrical internal courts. The entrance — placed centrally on the elongated travertine and brick front façade with a high, rusticated plinth — is rendered monumental by the entablature and high columns, reminiscent of an ancient temple. The garden elevation, on the other hand, is articulated by a series of high, imposing piers.

The layout of the internal spaces, both private rooms and reception areas, is governed by order and symmetry. The predominance of formal rigour and sober elegance seems to have anticipated the Neo-Classical taste that was to come. In actual fact, the buildings still conformed to Late Baroque tenants, as is clear from the theatrical plan for the project and the impressive octagonal vestibule in the main body of the building that measures over fifteen metres in diameter and is surrounded by twenty Doric columns, circular galleries and cupola. The exquisite Grand Staircase leads to the royal apartments and the Palatine Chapel. The central flight of stairs was carved from a single block of stone. The structural sophistication of this space, adorned with piers, cornices, arches and vaults as well as precious marbles, is one of the most splendid features of the Royal Palace.

opposite page, top left
Luigi Vanvitelli, aerial view of the Royal Palace of Caserta, begun 1752, Naples
The Royal Palace formed part of an urban restructuring plan geared to political, administrative and cultural requirements.

opposite page, top right
Luigi Vanvitelli, Palatine Chapel, Royal Palace of Caserta, begun 1752, Naples
The King wanted a chapel modelled on the chapel at the Royal Palace of Versailles. It is a large space with galleries and a colonnade resting on a tall plinth, adorned with precious marbles and gold decorations.

Luigi Vanvitelli, view of the Royal Palace of Caserta, begun 1752, Naples
Vanvitelli, was inspired by Bernini's projects for the Palais du Louvre and tried to lighten the compactness of the massive block by placing a projecting pavilion at each corner.

Other architectural gems include the small Court Theatre, built according to the model of San Carlo in Naples (1737). The theatre contains five levels of boxes with balustrades painted with cupids and garlands and high alabaster columns. The stage has an opening that could, when chosen, allow a glimpse of the outside world, creating a realistic effect of perspectival depth and landscape. Vanvitelli built an imposing aqueduct (Acqua Carolina) to supply water to the garden, built on a central axis terminating with the Royal Palace; its functionality demonstrates his considerable engineering skills. The water was transported to the Briano Hill before cascading down into the Fountain of Diana and Actaeon. The extraordinary vista of the long extended landscape, with the double avenue and fountains, remains to this day, culminating in the imposing Royal Palace.

Luigi Vanvitelli, view of the park, Royal Palace of Caserta, begun 1752, Naples
The waterway provides an elongated, telescopic perspective that slices through the hill as it flows towards the pool of the large waterfall.

LATE BAROQUE, SICILY

The earthquake that shook Sicily in January 1693 was nothing short of catastrophic: ancient and modern buildings, palaces and churches, simple homes, squares and streets were all devastated by its force. Thanks to the help of the Spanish government, town planners and architects were brought in to rebuild the city. The leading local architects had generally trained in Rome or had at least been there and assimilated the principles of 17th century Baroque. Great building yards were set up in Catania, Messina, Syracuse, Ragusa, Modica and Noto: the architecture that we admire today rose up from the ruins of that fateful day in 1693. Sicilian Late Baroque architecture was a clever fusion of Roman and Spanish Baroque combined with local traditional architecture, so Sicilian architecture developed a language of its own that emphasised theatrical qualities, with broad entry staircases, lively façades embellished with cornices, flamboyant ornamentation and an abundance of plastic elements, elegant balconies, interiors adorned with various marbles, frescoes and finely worked stuccoes. One of the major architects involved in this rush of building was Giovan Battista Vaccarini (1702–1768), a Sicilian who had trained in Rome. Vaccarini built the City Hall in Catania and the church of Sant'Agata (begun 1735), which was animated by a play of concave and convex elements inscribed in an elliptical plan. The city of Ragusa was rebuilt with two separate elements: a new district, with broad, straight roads built on a grid plan and the other built on the old site, reworked the old medieval urban fabric. The face of Ragusa changed irrevocably to become typically Late Baroque. This change is exemplified by the cathedral of San Giorgio, which started on site in 1739 according to plans drawn up by the architect, Rosario Gagliardi. Situated in a similar setting to the cathedral in Noto, San Giorgio also sits above a broad stairway and has a high, flamboyant façade animated by alternating concave and convex elements.

below, left
Pupil of Rosario Gagliardi, Modica Cathedral, begun 1730, Modica, Ragusa
Set above a spectacular stairway within the urban fabric of Ragusa, Modica Cathedral — with its imposing, monumental façade — is one of the highlights of Sicilian Baroque. The church was built to rival Rosario Gagliardi's San Giorgio Cathedral; it employs the façade: bell-tower pattern, in keeping with local custom.

below, right
Antonio Amato, detail of the decoration at Palazzo Biscari, begun 1707, Catania
The Prince of Biscari's palazzo was built over the rubble of the walls devastated by the earthquake. The palazzo looks out towards the ocean at Catania. The sculptor and architect, Antonio Amato of Messina, designed an intensely innovative and imaginative white stone cornice featuring stuccoes and festoons, volutes and masks.

THE MASTERPIECE
NOTO CATHEDRAL

The Cathedral in Noto is a masterpiece of Late Baroque Sicilian architecture. Like so many other churches and palaces, it was erected in the wake of the earthquake that had devastated much of eastern Sicily in January 1693.

The town of Noto was rebuilt eight kilometres away from the original settlement, largely by the architects, Rosario Gagliardi and Vincenzo Sinatra. Noto Cathedral is notable for the innovative solutions and the manner in which it adapts to the topography of the site, creating a considerably theatrical effect.

In the lower part of the city, where the centre of power and the institutions were located, the major buildings act as monumental nodes; these include the cathedral, built above a dramatic stairway.

The Church of San Nicolò, which became a cathedral in 1844, took decades of work and on-going reconstruction before its completion. Although the architect of the design is unknown, the identity of those who worked on the building are known. The cathedral was completely restored after the collapse of the cupola, nave and aisle, caused when the piers in the eastern aisle gave way.

External view of the Cathedral of San Nicolò, begun 1700, Noto, Syracuse
The broad sandstone façade is subdivided horizontally into two orders, in contrast there is one vertical central section and two side bell-towers that attenuate and enhance its appearance. The central section is crowned by a gable and adorned with columns and statues of the Evangelists. The large interior, with its Baroque chiaroscuro effects, contains a nave and two aisles. It is laid out in the shape of a Latin cross and crowned by a majestic cupola, which was rebuilt in 1870.

THE SPREAD OF ROCOCO

The early 18th century European landscape changed with the addition of luxurious royal palaces that replaced fortified castles and traditional palaces. Baroque brought about a new, far larger residential typology, developed wider façades laid out according to plans that were far more complex and dynamic, with multiple internal U-shaped courtyards with grand *cours d'honneur,* Courts of Honour and elaborate rear façades opening out onto large, theatrical parks adorned with pavilions. The Palais de Versailles, started in 1660 by Louis Le Vau and Jules Hardouin-Mansart, was the catalyst for the construction of a great many buildings from 1700 onwards and served as the supreme symbol of the absolute power and prestige of the sovereign.

The new, sophisticated aristocratic palaces contained private *appartements*, reception rooms as well as natural elements such as trees, plants, water features and fountains; the latter were even incorporated in urban residences.

Late Baroque palaces extended the traditional layout considerably with a central courtyard and created a few special spaces as 'jewels in the crown' of the palaces. For instance, the ballroom or reception rooms, which tended to be situated in the centre of the main body of the building. These more public spaces generally looked out onto a terrace with a panoramic view or faced directly into the garden. The entrance halls, with their lavish Grand Staircases, were built to welcome and impress guests.

During the Rococo period forms tended to be enormous and exaggerated, with an increasingly sophisticated play of curves and projections. The harmony of architecture, furnishings and landscape developed significantly during the Baroque period, reaching extraordinary heights with Rococo. Here, every element interacted with one another, to create a truly 'complete work of art' where creativity, variety and magnificence supersede function and reason.

Filippo Juvarra and Giovanni Battista
Sacchetti, Royal Palace, 1735—1764,
Madrid

Decorative and theatrical schemes took precedence in Rococo design, clad in wood or gilded stuccoes, ceramics and precious fabrics, where huge vaults were adorned with frescoes to astonishing illusionistic effect. The elliptical plan, so popular in Baroque churches, also featured in noble palaces; there were delightful studios and oval parlours which appeared unexpectedly behind doors tucked-away in corners. Rococo architecture signalled a move towards greater elegance, rather than the sumptuousness of Baroque. Rococo featured well-lit spaces decorated in pale colours such as azure, green or pink juxtaposed with the gold of stuccoes; there were also ample mirrors, which reflected reality in an infinite series of optical illusions, thus affecting the spatial perception of the spaces.

The Royal Palace and gardens at Versailles continued to seduce and fascinate sovereigns and aristocrats all over Europe for many years, even after they had lost their allure in Paris. The Royal Palace at Caserta, the Belvedere and Schönbrunn palaces in Vienna, and the Würzburg and Augustusburg Residences in Germany, are just a few examples of the extraordinarily high quality of projects that testify to the Late Baroque aspiration to create princely dwellings. The architects that were able to attain this height of achievement were numerous: men such as Luigi Vanvitelli, Balthasar Neumann, Johann Bernhard Fischer von Erlach, Johann Lucas von Hildebrandt and Francesco Bartolomeo Rastrelli.

Late Baroque architecture was adorned with an incredible variety of elements that conveyed impressions and meanings: its ability to beguile and astonish was so extraordinarily successful that Baroque soon spread beyond papal Rome to the far-flung corners of Europe. The message that was transmitted by art to subjects throughout Europe and the colonies abroad was devotion to God and allegiance to the sovereign. The grandeur and opulence of Late Baroque advanced even further: signalling a strong and determined desire to overturn the limitations of Classicism and traditional codes to discover new expressions and to challenge the technical boundaries and methods inherited by previous generations. During their

below, left
Balthasar Neumann and Giambattista Tiepolo, Imperial Hall, 1720–1752, Würzburg Residence, Germany
In the Imperial Hall in Würzburg, Neumann achieved a harmonious and balanced 'spectacle of light' which served as the central focus of the palace: the octagonal Kaisesaal, with its wealth of marble, sculpture, stucco-work and frescoes. The relatively simple structure consists of a series of fluted columns supporting the vault, interpenetrated by large apertures on the diagonals and the main axis. Tiepolo depicted medieval episodes from the history of the city of Würzburg on the interior of the theatrical space decorated with white and gilded stuccoes, which were selected by the Prince-Bishop in order to emphasise the historical legitimacy of his power.

below, right
Miguel Cabrera, altarpiece dedicated to St. Francis Xavier, 1753, Jesuit church, Tepotzotlán, Mexico
The monumental complex in Tepotzotlán is representative of the 'new' Spanish culture and dissemination of Baroque art.

extensive travels, Late Baroque architects observed and analysed what they saw, to then reformulate their attained knowledge, at times blending it with local traditions, to create their own new increasingly bold and sophisticated architectural vocabulary.

An incredibly versatile language thus spread to numerous countries, including the colonies ruled by Catholic monarchies, such as Spain and Portugal. The missionary activity in the Americas exported priests and preachers as well as the aesthetic Baroque code, which became even more influential than before in these new surroundings.

Hispano-American architecture in the 18th century produced surprisingly beautiful buildings where the decorative concept took precedence over the architectural/spatial element, to form a powerful missionary tool for the evangelists. Jesuits, Dominicans and Franciscans all built large-scale grand churches at the centres of their missions, which over the course of a few years, developed into genuine cities.

The Jesuit model was clearly inspired by the prototype of the 'mother' church in Rome, which had a generous nave with a side pulpit for the preacher. Many decorative elements, unknown in European churches, began to emerge: references to local culture, indigenous customs and symbolic forms.

Trees and garlands laden with tropical fruit became the backdrop for the most common repertoire of Christian images. Colonial Late Baroque is characterised by extraordinary opulence and dynamism: façades, portals and retables were all transformed into rare, precious works of art. The unrestrained use of bright colours was made possible thanks to the variety of stone, ceramics and coloured stuccoes.

Jacob Prandtauer and Joseph Munggenast, view of the vault of the church at the Abbey of Melk, 1702–1736, Austria
The theatrical effect of the exterior of the Abbey of Melk, set high above the Danube River, is also recreated within the church.

THE HAPSBURG EMPIRE: A STATE ART

After suppressing the Ottoman siege of 1683, the Hapsburg dynasty took up its permanent residence in Vienna: the empire was preparing for the new century as a rapidly expanding territorial and economic power. Charles VI (1711–1740) encouraged the blossoming of the arts and architecture with the arrival of numerous artists from far-afield, who used Late Baroque as a medium to express the power of the Imperial crown. Palaces and churches designed by great architects such as Fischer von Erlach and Johann Lucas Hildebrandt were constructed all over Austria; feverish building activities rapidly changed the face of Vienna into a worthy rival to Paris. These new buildings were clearly influenced by the work of 17th century Italian architects such as Bernini and Borromini, as well as some of their pupils, like for instance, Carlo Fontana, who served as a role model for Fischer von Erlach and Hildebrandt. Unlike Germany, which was largely Protestant, Austrian Late Baroque architecture was influenced to a great degree by Italian religious architecture. The Hapsburg Empire, which supported Orthodox Roman Catholicism, asserted its own prestige by restoring many sacred buildings: the State-Church union was a fundamental factor in guaranteeing the stability of the absolute government. French-style Rococo also found fertile ground in the decoration of interiors, with decorators and cabinet-makers, most of whom came from Italy. The Imperial Summer Palace of Schönbrunn (1696–1711), conceived as a Hapsburg version of Versailles, contained rooms from different periods, the most exquisite of which were decorated in flamboyant Rococo style.

Johann Lucas von Hildebrandt, Palais Kinsky, 1713–1716, Vienna
The palace reveals its architect's penchant for lively, articulated and richly decorated façades. The pilasters on the slightly projecting central section are tapered on the *piano nobile*; the upper floor window surrounds alternate with three semicircular mouldings set between two pointed surrounds on either side. Palais Kinsky is one of the most accomplished and modern examples of 18th century European civil architecture.

JOHANN BERNHARD FISCHER VON ERLACH

The Austrian architect, Johann Bernhard Fischer von Erlach (1656–1723) was the most brilliant exponent of Hapsburg Late Baroque. Trained as a sculptor and stucco decorator, he worked in Rome and Naples and was able to reformulate the teachings of Bernini, Borromini and Fontana into his own personal, elegant and exuberant style. Fischer von Erlach was erudite and highly regarded; by his thirties he had already been granted the prestigious right to use the noble suffix 'von' in his name. In 1693, as part of the celebratory Hapsburg Empire building programme, he was commissioned to build a palace outside Vienna for Leopold I. The palace was to replace a castle damaged by the Turks in battle and was to be modelled on the sumptuous Palais de Versailles. The new, rather less lavish and flamboyant Palace of Schönbrunn (1696–1711) remains one of the most elegant Imperial residences of the 18th century.

Fischer von Erlach's final grandiose scheme for the Court Library in Vienna was completed by his son, Joseph Emanuel — who succeeded him as Court Architect — following his death in 1723. The majestic elliptical space is an sophisticated demonstration of Imperial prestige, with its magnificent precious woods, marbles, stuccoes and frescoes.

Fischer von Erlach also undertook the challenging task of writing the first monumental illustrated history of architecture (*Entwurf einer Historischen Architektur*, 1721), which even covers Egyptian and Chinese architecture. The publication was to have a considerable influence on the design of subsequent exotic architectural elements.

Johann Bernhard Fischer von Erlach, exterior of the Karlskirche, 1715–1721, Vienna
Fischer von Erlach's religious masterpiece was the church dedicated to St Charles (1715–1721) in Vienna, which was unique in the Hapsburg repertoire: clearly drawn from the monuments the architect had studied in Rome: from the Pantheon to Trajan's Column and the church of Sant'Agnese. Fischer von Erlach's work was fundamentally and recurringly Baroque. In this church, the oval, surmounted by a cupola, is a clear combination of centralisation and extension. His work shows that he was determined to create 'historical architecture' that looked to past architectural achievements and reinterpreted them into new and original forms.

THE MASTERPIECE
BELVEDERE PALACE

Towards the end of the 17th century, Fischer von Erlach designed a summer palace on the outskirts of Vienna for Prince Eugene of Savoy, a heroic General in the Hapsburg Army. The Prince was not entirely satisfied with the design and thus, subsequently commissioned the Italian-trained architect Johann Lucas von Hildebrandt (1668–1745), who had developed a more decorative and refined style. Von Hildebrandt's design, which provided for a palace with a Grand Courtyard and large terraced garden, was situated on an elongated, slightly inclined site. In 1720 von Hildebrandt suggested the creation of a second palace on the opposite side of the garden, which would have an elevated position and an enchanting view over the Hapsburg capital. Seen from the 'Lower' Belvedere, the new building (known as the 'Upper' Belvedere, completed in 1723) was a spectacular architectural backdrop, sitting above the long terraced garden. The exterior spaces were designed to blend elegantly as well as functionally with the residential ones. The Upper Belvedere has an imposing triple-arched central entrance, crowned with a majestic curved gable, a rhythmic series of broad windows, terminating on both ends with corner towers capped with low domes.

The roof of the palace is enlivened by the varying heights of the building volumes. Although the palace is fairly uniform, there was a clear attempt to break away from the traditional tenets of order and symmetry. The architectural vocabulary is less formal and more playful. The structure as a whole is both elaborate and elegant, featuring a wealth of plastic ornamentation. The beautifully articulated and theatrical Belvedere complex exemplifies the penchant that architects of the Late Baroque had for new, unusual harmonies where the gardens and palaces interact, complementing and affirming one another in a continual cross-reference of analogies and contrasts.

Johann Lucas von Hildebrandt, views of the façades of the Upper Belvedere Palace, 1721–1723, Vienna
Von Hildebrandt planned a scheme of volumes of varying shapes in the Upper Palace, like an ensemble of festive pavilions. The play of window openings — no longer governed by the traditional pattern of orders — the elegant curves of the gables and the small corner domes, the varying heights and the cornices, make this palace one of the most accomplished blend of the numerous architectural codes of the period. The enormous terrace to the rear opens out onto an incredible view of the Viennese cityscape, while the sloping garden falls away to meet the less complex Lower Belvedere Palace.

The Upper Belvedere Palace was used for parties and receptions. Guests would enter through the Grand Courtyard at the Lower Belvedere and advance through the garden, with the splendid reflection of the Upper Palace mirrored in the lake. The original garden layout was planned to progress upwards from the Lower Palace. Thus the main hall in the Lower Belvedere (the Marble Hall), with its myriad of marbles, stuccoes and paintings, was used as a reception room for the most important guests.

THE ABBEYS OF JACOB PRANDTAUER

Very few abbeys outside Austria are as splendid or refined, either architecturally or artistically, as those built in Austria. Ambitious projects were drawn up for restructuring the ancient medieval abbeys, transforming them into quasi Imperial Palaces in keeping with the religious and political Hapsburg approach; rooted in the Holy Roman Empire. The powerful Abbots, who descended from noble families, not only had vast financial resources, but also shared the princely passion for huge ambitious projects. The bulk of monastic architecture at the time was designed by sculptors and stonemasons, guided by the knowledgeable Abbots, rather than by refined Court Architects. The Tyrolean sculptor, Jacob Prandtauer (1660–1726), belonged to this category. Later in his career, he devoted himself largely to architecture, building the most elaborate of all abbeys, Melk Abbey. Along with Fischer von Erlach and Hildebrandt, Prandtauer achieved the greatest heights of Austrian Late Baroque architecture. He also built St Florian Abbey, near Linz, which is considered to be the most important Late Baroque monastery in Upper Austria. The complex is arranged around one larger and two smaller courtyards. The church is inspired by Il Gesù in Rome, and consists of a space divided into four-bays with women's galleries and side chapels, as well as a dome over the crossing. The high, double-tower façade is connected to the western elevation, where the main entrance foyer is situated. Prandtauer also designed the church at Sonntagberg (1706–1717), which is reminiscent of a smaller-scale Melk Abbey, as well as the church at Dürnstein (1716), situated on the Danube. The abbey was transformed by Prandtauer and features more compact versions of the towers and terrace overlooking the River Melk.

Jacob Prandtauer, Marble Hall, St Florian Abbey, 1708–1724, Linz, Austria
Carlo Antonio Carlone had embarked on a new design for the Augustinian abbey in 1686; in 1708, after Carlone's death, Prandtauer took over the project management of the site, which continued until 1724. The monastery acquired an elegant and palatial appearance, featuring a splendid vaulted staircase (*Treppenhaus*) and the magnificent Marble Hall with alternating large windows and pairs of high, coloured marble columns. The elegant reception hall exemplifies the decorative and pictorial exuberance that characterises the entire abbey. Prandtauer inserted the lavish Marble Hall into a wing that extends beyond the perimeter of the monastery. His concept was to establish a strong iconographic link between the hall and the Abbey church: symbolising the triumph of Faith in the church and the triumph over Disbelief. The fresco on the vault, by Martino Altomonte (1658–1745), depicts the triumph of Price Eugene of Savoy over the Turks, thereby exalting both Imperial power and the power of the Church.

THE MASTERPIECE
MELK ABBEY

Melk Abbey lies along the banks of the Danube River, north-west of Vienna. Its renown is connected with the imposing Benedictine Abbey that dominates the town. The Babenburg princes chose the rocky peninsular above the Danube as their home as early as around 1,000 AD and a century or so later Margrave Leopold II founded a Benedictine monastery on the site with monks from Lambach Monastery (Upper Austria), famous for its scriptorium. The architect, Jacob Prandtauer, embarked on the restoration of Melk Abbey in 1702, which is one of the largest Baroque monastic complexes. Due to its dominant position overlooking the Danube, the abbey is unique and impressive. The complex looks rather like a gigantic flotilla stretching across the promontory towards the river. The southern elevation is 250-metres-long and resembles a princely palace. The reconstruction began with the

church and its twin-tower façade over the river. A semicircular gallery around the façade of the church links the two wings containing the library and the Marble Hall. The architecture echoes the contours of the rocky outcrop, reminiscent of ancient fortifications. The interior of the church consists of a single space, with women's galleries on the upper floor, above which the luminous drum and cupola open out.

The extraordinary location of the building meant that Prandtauer was inspired to indulge his talents as a sculptor and architect to the full. Prandtauer's scheme was eventually completed by his nephew, Joseph Munggenast in 1736. Numerous artists, including the painters, Johann Michael Rottmayr and Paul Troger, the stuccoist, Johann Pöckh and the architect and interior designer, Antonio Beduzzi, also worked on the project.

Jacob Prandtauer and Joseph Munggenast, view of the exterior of Melk Abbey, 1702–1736, Austria
The Benedictine Melk Abbey was the most scenic of all the abbeys, poised on top of a rocky outcrop overlooking the Danube River. The salient parts of the complex are situated towards the river: the panoramic semicircular gallery, the rooftop loggia, the two wings containing the Marble Hall and the library, the façade of the church held between two bell-towers, the high cupola and the longitudinal development of the monastic apartments. The closely-knit articulation of the volumes, the symbolic centrality of the church and the chiaroscuro effects of the ochre and white walls are all typical of Rococo architecture.

PRAGUE AND MORAVIA

Prague witnessed an extraordinary architectural renaissance during the 18th century. The taste for Baroque — initially imported by Italian and French architects and artists — took on its own specific character in Bohemia. To this day this development is evident in the region's architectural landscape. The architecture produced in Prague was strikingly elegant and theatrical, yet never excessively or opulently so. Prague thus became the Late Baroque city *par excellence* in Central Europe, dotted with palaces and churches, sculptures and plastic decorations, bridges and gardens. The primary patrons of this sophisticated Baroque renewal were the Dientzenhofer family from the Bavarian Alps, who managed to blend the Italian Baroque vocabulary with various Bavarian architectural quirks, creating an internationally-famous architectural model that was to be emulated throughout Central Europe. Christoph Dientzenhofer (1655–1722) built his greatest works in Prague; works such as the church of St Nicholas; its façade characterised by the movement and play of concave-convex shapes, clearly inspired by Borromini. The star of Bohemian Baroque architecture was, however, Christoph's son, Kilian Ignaz Dientzenhofer (1690–1751). His major works include the choir and cupola of the church of St Nicholas, where his emphatically Rococo style, his love of helixes and undulating movement stood out prominently among the work of his more Classical contemporaries. A great many noble palaces were built in Prague; they were surrounded by elegant gardens, or revamped in the new Rococo style. The famous, medieval Charles Bridge was constructed and decorated with splendid Late Baroque sculptures of saints by Matyás Braun and Ferdinand Maxmilián Brokoff.

Kilian Ignaz Dientzenhofer, Kinsky Palace, 1755–1765, Prague
A part of Prague's history is conserved in the buildings that surround the Old City Square. The square is dominated by the church of St Nicholas and Kinsky Palace, which has a delightful Rococo façade embellished with stuccoes by Bossi as well as statues of the four earthly elements, executed in 1760–1765 by Ignaz Franz Platzer. Stépán Kinsky, an Imperial diplomat, acquired the palace from the Goltz family in 1768.

THE MASTERPIECE
CHURCH OF ST NICHOLAS

The Church of St Nicolas was designed during the frenzy of building that changed the
elegant 15th–16th century city-scape of
Prague into the capital of Bohemian Baroque.
The numerous newly-built churches were
intended to testify to the victory of Hapsburg
Catholicism over Protestantism. The church
belonged to the Jesuit order and was built in
the heart of the Malá Strana district, where
since the Middle Ages there had been a place
of worship dedicated to St Nicholas. Construction started in 1703 under Christoph
Dientzenhofer and was resumed by his son,
Kilian Ignaz, after his death in 1722. The
church was not fully completed until three
decades later, in 1752. The double order on
the façade, with vertical concave and convex
elements, is crowned by the great curved
gable, in a very sophisticated Late Baroque
vocabulary that confers an air of theatricality
to the building both internally and externally.

**Christoph and Kilian Ignaz Dientzenhofer,
exterior view of the Church of
St Nicholas, 1703–1752, Prague**

PLAGUE COLUMNS

A typically Late Baroque element characteristic of many squares in central Eastern Europe, is the so-called 'plague column', dedicated to the Virgin Mary or the Holy Trinity, erected between the late 17th and early 18th centuries. The column as a commemorative monument (previously seen in Ancient Rome) returned to fashion during the Baroque era, especially within the confines of the Hapsburg Empire. Plague columns, were imbued with a wealth of symbolic meanings and created an elegant visual focus in city squares that tended to be centrally-located hubs of activity. Horrific medieval plague epidemics continued to break out for centuries, largely spread along the great trade routes. During the late 17th century in Austria and early 18th century in Moravia, there were a large number of epidemics. This led to a great many plague columns being erected in Hapsburg cities between 1680 and 1750, becoming one of the singular expressions of Late Baroque Catholicism in these particular regions. Liberation from plague epidemics was frequently associated with the liberation from the threat of Ottoman occupation, subsequent to the thwarted Vienna siege of 1683. The most noteworthy plague columns are: the *Pestsäule* (plague column, 1692) in Vienna — which soars up in the heart of the Grabenplatz (square) — and the Holy Trinity Column (1716–1754) at Olomouc, considered to be one of the finest Late Baroque sculptures in the Czech Republic. Other plague columns worthy of note include: the column in Prague (1715); the Austrian columns in Klagenfurt (1680) and Linz (1723); the Slovenian column at Skofja Loka (1751); the Slovakian column in Nitra (1750) and the Hungarian column in Budapest (1713).

below, left
Giovanni Battista Aliprandi, Plague Column, 1715, Prague
Two plague columns were built in Prague: this particular one, designed by Giovanni Battista Aliprandi in 1715, is situated in St Nicholas Square in Malá Strana. Powerless to prevent or combat the awful epidemics — regarded as manifestations of divine wrath — communities held dramatic processions, imploring for divine forgiveness as they erected their votive columns.

below, right
Johann Bernhard Fischer von Erlach and Paul Strudel, Plague Column, 1687–1692, Vienna
The plague column in Vienna derives from a pledge made by Emperor Leopold I in 1679, imploring for an end to the terrible pestilence afflicting the region. Hans Frühwirth built a temporary wooden column, replaced with an imposing monument commissioned by Matthias Rauchmiller and later remodelled by Johann Bernhard Fischer von Erlach and Lodovico Ottavio Burnacini. Dedicated to the Holy Trinity, the column has a three-sided base with reliefs of Biblical episodes and a suggestive allegory of Faith triumphing over the plague. The marble column rises from the centre, becoming enclosed by marble clouds bearing splendid sculpted figures aloft.

opposite page
Václav Render and Andreas Zahner, Holy Trinity Column, consecrated in 1754, Olomuc, Czech Republic
The Holy Trinity Column in Olomouc was conceived by the sculptor Václav Render, who dreamed of creating a truly unique and imposing monument. Unfortunately Render died several years before the column was eventually consecrated.

BERLIN: A NEW CAPITAL

Thanks to the House of Hohenzollern, social and political conditions in Branden-burg, the future heart of Prussia, improved considerably during the early 18th cen-tury. Art and architecture started to bourgeon and a lengthy period of prosperity began under Frederick I (1657–1713) – who became the first King of Prussia in 1701 – Frederick William (1688–1740) and particularly under the enlightened ruler, Frederick the Great (1712–1786), who reigned from 1740 onwards. As architecture was the most direct and effective means of signalling their prestige, the sovereigns decided to establish new building yards. Baroque was naturally the most appropri-ate architectural language for expressing the magnificence of the new nation. Palaces went up in Berlin, a network of roads and boulevards were laid out and extension work also started on the thoroughfare, Unter den Linden in 1701. The old Berliner Stadtschloss, (subsequently destroyed) was rebuilt in the new Baroque style by Andreas Schlüter in 1698. The project was later assigned to Court Archi-tect, Friedrich Eosander von Göthe in 1707. The castle was the official residence of the Kings (later Emperors) of Prussia for over two centuries, between 1701 and 1918. In 1701, construction work also began on Lietzenburg Palace, a few kilome-tres outside of Berlin. The palace had been built by Arnold Nering as a summer residence and was converted by von Göthe into a luxurious villa. After the sudden death of the young Queen, Sophia Charlotte in 1705, Frederick I renamed it 'Char-lottenburg' in her honour.

façade and courtyard of Charlottenburg Castle, 1695–1712, Berlin
The castle building recalls its prede-cessor, Versailles, though extended into a U-shaped layout, where the Court of Honour opens out towards the city. Bordering the rear façade is an enormous French-inspired garden with orthogonal paths that circulate the planted terraces and the water feat-ures. In around 1712 the main body of the castle was completed with a tym-panum and a high Baroque dome.

Georg Wenzeslaus von Knobelsdorff,
Golden Gallery (top) and Porcelain
Cabinet (left) at the Castle of Charlottenburg, begun 1740, Berlin
The interior of the castle is typically
Rococo with regard to its use of stuccoes, mirrors and gilding. The Porcelain Cabinet is renowned for its splendid collection of *chinoiseries*, displayed
on the walls like precious decorative
artefacts. It is also well-known for the
magnificent Banqueting Hall, over forty
metres long, known as the 'Golden Gallery', embellished with putti and gilded
stuccoes of shells, flowers and fruit
layered over the green plasterwork.

THE MASTERPIECE
SANSSOUCI

left
Georg Wenzeslaus von Knobelsdorff,
Music Room, Sanssouci Palace,
1745–1750, Potsdam, Germany
The two arms of the building, extending out from the *corps de logis*, contain the private rooms, library and study. The Music Room is heavily decorated in highly ornate Rococo white and gold stuccoes and paintings; large mirrors reflect the garden view from the windows back into the room in a fantastic play of cross-references.

Potsdam, approximately thirty kilometres southwest of Berlin, underwent considerable expansion between 1722 and 1740, after having been decreed the permanent garrison of the King's troops. Frederick II commissioned Court Architect, Georg Wenzeslaus von Knobelsdorff (1699–1753), to build the Sanssouci Palace in 1745. The first sketch designs were drawn by the King himself, who was passionate about architecture. Sanssouci Palace is one of the finest examples of French-style Rococo; even its name *sans souci*, which is French for 'carefree', conveys the Baroque ethos of frivolity. The palace was originally built as a retreat where the King could spend the summer months and indulge his personal interests far from courtly duties. Frederick II's original idea was to build a large, terraced vineyard on the hill; he intended to create a kind of Arcadia as was fashionable in France, however he eventually decided to build a private residence. Thus a grand single-storey palace was built, surrounded by curved terraces planted with vines and fruit trees. The King stipulated that the interior and the exterior floor level of the palace were to be flush, with no need for steps or stairs, as he wanted to be able to access the gardens directly from his room. Knobelsdorff had studied both the Italian Renaissance and contemporary French art and was thus able to design a residence of careful and well-dimensioned proportions. The design was also greatly influenced by the latest Rococo style; its interior spaces are elegant and grandiose. Despite the sophistication of the rooms, the palace is not over elaborate; its atmosphere reflects the intimate nature of the King's 'private' pleasures. Although the palace might have been for the King's private use, Sanssouci was nevertheless very grand: on arrival, guests would advance along the fine Corinthian colonnade to the *cour d'honneur*. The vestibule was allocated to the centre of the building, with its columns, gilded stuccoes and frescoed vault. The luminous, oval Marble Hall, surmounted by an elliptical cupola, forms the focal point of the palace; this space is also covered with gilded stuccoes and is lit from above, vaguely recalling the Pantheon in Rome. Splendid precious marble intarsia, clusters of flowers and floral motifs enliven the pale stone floor and the large French doors confer a spacious feel, while providing a splendid view over the gardens and the vineyards.

**Georg Wenzeslaus von Knobelsdorff,
Garden Façade, Sanssouci
1745–1750, Potsdam, Germany**
The great terraced vineyards were built on convex curves to make maximum use of daylight hours, as well as to echo the form of the great Baroque stairways. A long flight of steps leads down from the terraces, culminating in a terrace with a large water basin with fountains. In addition to the terraced vineyard, Frederick II also commissioned a large park with a two-kilometre-long central avenue. The park is dotted with statues, *tempietti* and follies in true Rococo style.

DRESDEN: CITY OF WONDERS

Subsequent to a fire in 1685 which destroyed Dresden, the capital of Saxony, frenetic building activity was triggered, transforming the city into a veritable treasure chest of new buildings. Overseen by Court Architects on both sides of the River Elba, a huge town plan was drawn up, which culminated in the Zwinger Palace. One of the major projects built during this era was the Frauenkirche, the city's main Protestant church. The Frauenkirche is quintessentially Baroque; differing from other contemporary Southern German churches with its compact central plan and theatrical layout. The church was designed by the architect, George Bähr and was built between 1726 and 1743. Utterly destroyed by Allied bombing in 1945, meticulous and painstaking reconstruction work began forty-five years later, in 1990, and the church was eventually reopened to the public in 2005. The Roman Catholic Cathedral, Hofkirche is not situated very far from the Frauenkirche. The cathedral was built for Frederick Augustus II, Elector of Saxony, who had converted to Catholicism in 1719 and wanted his city to have a Catholic church near to the Protestant church. Hofkirche was built by the Roman architect, Gaetano Chiavari, between 1738 and 1755. Chiaveri – who had already worked in St Petersburg and Warsaw – was well versed in both Italian and Northern European architecture. His design for the church was large-scale with a high Gothic tower on the façade; seen from the opposite bank of the River Elba, it was to serve as the ideal focal point of the cityscape. The church has a nave and two aisles; its dynamic curved shapes are echoed on the façade; it is surrounded by a high balustrade on which seventy-eight figures of saints, sculpted by Lorenzo Mattielli, are displayed.

below, left
Gaetano Chiaveri, Hofkirche, 1738–1755, Dresden, Germany
The Roman architect, Gaetano Chiaveri, built the church at one end of the Augustus Bridge in order to counterbalance the Protestant Frauenkirche on the other end, thus symbolising the sovereign's dual role as both Catholic King and Protestant Prince-Elector. Chiaveri inserted a high, Gothic-like tower which – when viewed from the riverbank – is situated directly at the point where the axes between the castle and the Zwinger intersect. The nave of the church is orientated towards the city; both the East and West ends of the building are rounded.

below, centre and right
George Bähr, exterior view and plan of the Frauenkirche, 1722–1743, Dresden, Germany
The original 1722 scheme was designed as a Greek cross plan with tribunes surmounted by an imposing dome. Bähr later changed his design to have a circle of piers held within a square plan with and four small corner towers above the dome, which emphasise the verticality and makes the composition look elegant and slender. The raised choir can be accessed by two spectacular, curved stairways.

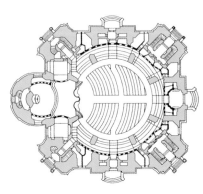

THE MASTERPIECE
THE ZWINGER PALACE

The East German city of Dresden was transformed into a massive Late Baroque building site during the early 18th century: *'Dresdner Barock'*, the particular, refined urban style, was only to wane with the devastation wrought by the Seven Years' War (1756–1763). The leading architect of the period, Matthäus Daniel Pöppelmann (1662–1736), was first appointed as General Building Superintendent and then subsequently as Court Architect. Pöppelmann was fascinated by the extraordinary architectural possibilities of Italian Baroque and was able to formulate his own refined and carefully measured style, creating extremely emotive works; the most famous of which is the Zwinger Palace. Situated on the site of the ancient fortress bastions, the Zwinger served as a prestigious arena for festivals, tournaments and games, as well as an exhibition space. The palace was not used as the residence of the Princes of Saxony. Augustus the Strong (1694–1733) built it as a spectacular venue containing pavilions, fountains and stairways. Pöppelmann had in fact built a tim-

ber structure in the square where an official festival and grand banquet was to be held on the occasion of an official visit from the King of Denmark, in 1709. Immediately after the grand occasion a double-storey sandstone pavilion, known as the *'Wallpavillon'* — which has two spectacular galleries that lead off from it, culminating in corner pavilions. The entire complex is clearly inspired by the French tribunes from which the nobility used to watch jousting matches: the pavilion is a broad, monumental enclosure, along which open and closed blocks were erected, that house priceless museum collections today. The central, double-storey pavilion is sumptuously and elaborately decorated with a wealth of sculptural figures. It is regarded as the sculptor, Balthasar Permoser's finest work. The Zwinger was inaugurated in 1719 on the occasion of the wedding of Frederick Augustus II, Elector of Saxony, to the daughter of the Austrian Emperor, Maria Josepha of Hapsburg. The complex was subsequently enlarged; only parts of it escaped destruction during the Second World War.

Matthäus Daniel Pöppelmann, Zwinger Palace, 1709–1728, Dresden, Germany
The Zwinger (which literally means 'dungeon', given that it is built in the space between the city fortifications) is a unique and highly creative model within the realm of rhetorical architecture. The huge, roughly square, space has a concave U-shape on the transversal axis and is surrounded by a single-storey gallery that is linked to the double-storey pavilions on either side.

THE TRIUMPH OF ROCOCO: BAVARIA

During the first half of the 18th century, architecture – religious architecture in particular — experienced a particularly fervent renaissance in Bavaria, giving rise to one of the most sophisticated architectural vocabularies in Europe. Catholic Bavaria, which bordered onto territories that were predominantly Protestant, harnessed the seductive and flamboyant Late Baroque and Rococo vocabulary to affirm its own power and prestige. Churches and monasteries had to radiate beauty and opulence and create representative buildings on a par with the civil glory of the noblility's princely residences. In stark contrast to places of worship in North Central Germany that symbolised frugality and direct contact to God as preached by the Protestant reform, the Catholic tradition in Bavaria chose rather to produce works of extraordinary architectural originality and decorative wealth. The close proximity of Bavaria to France and Italy made it easier for skilled artisans and artists to communicate and share their ideas, thus a great number of Italian artists worked closely with local Bavarian artists in Northern European principalities. While the stark Northern churches did not lend themselves to particular heights of creativity, in Bavaria the need to build new, sumptuous places of worship encouraged the spread of the flamboyant Rococo vocabulary, culminating in exquisite and at times rather kitsch interiors such as the saccharine Wieskirche in Steingaden and the flamboyant churches at Rohr and Ottobeuren. A characteristic specific to Bavarian churches is the difference between the external and internal structure of the buildings. The interiors of the luminous Rococo churches are highly theatrical and dynamic and offer a myriad of different perspectives to admire as one moves around the spaces inside them.

Johann Michael Fischer, façade and view of the interior of the Abbey church at Ottobeuren, 1748–1766, Germany
A masterpiece of Bavarian Rococo, the church of the ancient Benedictine Abbey at Ottobeuren is an astonishing blend of architectural structure and decorative refinement that alter the perception of the spaces which are enlivened by furnishings and sculptures. The exterior of the church is rather sober, with dynamic curvilinear contours, while inside the building the spatial effect is focused on the intersection which is surmounted by a powerful dome. Ottobeuren Abbey is a reinterpretation of the traditional centrally-planned basilica with a broad transept, choir and side chapels.

THE ASAM BROTHERS

The Asam brothers used spatial illusion as an optical device pushed to the limits in the service of the Catholic faith. Born into an artistic family (their father, Hans Georg was a renowned fresco painter), Cosmas Damian (1686–1739) and Egid Quirin (1692–1750) were in the artistic vanguard of the great Rococo style in the Northern European Catholic areas, especially in Southern Germany. Inspired by Italian 17th century architecture, the brothers managed to achieve a wonderful interplay of architecture, sculpture and painting. As the brothers were architects, painters, sculptors and stuccoists themselves, they were able to translate the flamboyant Late Baroque taste for theatricality into exuberant, mesmerising works. Most of their projects were grand abbeys, for which they were responsible for the architectural reconstruction as well as the interior decoration. With their skills and knowledge, they were able to achieve a superb sense of continuity with sculptures, stuccoes, frescoes and furnishings. After the death of their father, the Asam brothers spent a couple of years in Rome between 1711 and 1713, where they studied the great Baroque buildings. The brothers were particularly fascinated by the masterpieces of Bernini and Borromini, as well as the 17th century illusionistic art of Pietro da Cortona, Andrea Pozzo and Carlo Maratta. On their return to Germany, Cosmas Damian concentrated on painting, while Egid Quirin sculpted; creating altars, ensembles of statues as well as ornamental stuccoes. The two brothers managed to build perspectively perfect illusionistic spaces; thus making the enclosed interiors of churches seem far larger by using the architectural structures to emphasise the upward thrust. Furthermore, they took advantage of sculptures, pictorial decorations and the play of light to create a spectacular, ethereal kind of space. The major works of the Asam brothers include: the Abbey church in Weltenburg (1716), Church of the Ascension in Aldersbach (c. 1721), the Abbey church in Rohr (1721–1723), as well as St John Nepomuceno in Munich (1733– 1746).

below, left
Nave of the Church of the Ascension, c. 1721, Aldersbach, Germany
This Abbey in Aldersbach is a true treasure-chest of art works, executed by many of the greatest artists involved in Southern Late Baroque; like Bartholmäus Altomonte, Matthäus Günther, Christian Wink and Griessmann – the cabinet-maker who created the side altars. The vault frescoes of the early 18th century in Germany illustrate a rejection of formal restraints and an embrace of frivolous gaiety.

below, right
The High Altar, Church of the Agostinian Monastery 1723, Rohr, Germany
This imposing architectural, sculptural and ornamental high altar, which is dedicated to the Assumption of the Virgin, achieves great theatrical heights of expression. The spectacular gilded stuccoes in white and gold dazzle, the figures are modelled with elegance and expertise and the drapery is animated with vigorous plasticity.

THE MASTERPIECE
ST JOHN NEPOMUCENO

Entirely planned, built and funded by the Asam brothers, the Church of St John Nepomuceno in Munich, also known as the Asamkirche, is a unique example of the synergy between client and architect. Between 1729 and 1730, Egid Quirin Asam acquired a number of properties in Sendlingerstrasse, where he intended to build residences; whilst at the same time his brother, Cosmas Damian, bought the site on which the church was later to be built. In this small gem of a church, the architecture and interior decoration are merged to such a degree that they manage to achieve a rare balance that underpins the concept of the *Gesamtkunstwerk* (total work of art). The dramatic illusions and spatial effects created are further enhanced by the skilful use of light and other Baroque techniques

gleaned from their studies in Rome. Despite the restricted available space in the church, the Asam brothers managed to incorporate tortile columns, elegant balusters and vertical galleries decorated with gilded stucco arabesques and frescoes. The nave opens out into a dramatic space which terminates in a barrel vault lit by two apertures. The church testifies to the Asam brothers' mastery of Roman optical illusions created by perspectival decoration.

The brothers' sheer skill with regard to grafting a large variety of shapes in restricted spaces can be compared with Borromini's mastery of sculpting forms in space. The interior of the church is like a *'Berniniesque theatrum sacrum'*; a harmonious synthesis of architecture, sculpture and painting.

above, left
Cosmas Damian and Egid Quirin Asam, view of the exterior of St John Nepomuceno, 1733–1734, Munich
The double-storey façade of the Asam Church forms a convex curve; it has a portal with columns and a broad window opening. There is no clue on the exterior to hint at, or suggest, the wealth of ornamentation to be discovered around the nave inside.

above, right
Cosmas Damian Asam and Egid Quirin Asam, view of the interior of St John Nepomuceno, 1733–1736, Munich
The interior of the church is high and narrow with a single nave. The interior benefits enormously from being arranged on two floors, emphasised by the fiercely projecting mouldings and the perspectival paintings of St John with his trademark gesture.

THE IMPERIAL RESIDENCE

The most significant urban planning developments occurring in German-speaking regions during the 18th century were the extension of smaller, regional town centres. In some instances new towns were planned, whilst in other cases, existing towns were transformed and the Court transported beyond the confines of the city. The nobility in Germany desired grandiose castles that symbolised their power and might. The magnificent and imposing residences were designed to symbolise the political and financial clout of the sovereign. So-called 'Imperial Residences' were extended around the court to incorporate administrative and auxiliary buildings that were often to evolve over time as cities. An example of such a residence was Wittelsbacher in Munich. On occasion both counterpoints remained — residence and city — the residence might have been established within the city walls or else in the midst of an already existing city. Elsewhere residences were built according to the prototypes of 17th century Paris and Versailles where the castle was relocated to the perimeter of the city. This was the case in various residences in Germnay like Berlin's Lietzenburg (later Charlottenburg) or Stuttgart's Ludwigsburg, Mannheim's Schwetzingen, München's Nymphenburg and Kassel's Wilhelmshöhe. Rococo Imperial residences are real architectural gems that embody the high ambitions of the noble patrons who commissioned the most renowned architects to translate their wishes in the most creative fashion possible. The architects not only created sumptuous halls, courts and stairways, but also gardens and enormous parks with intricate terraces, nymphs, fountains and water features, perfectly orthogonal pathways, woodlands and fruit orchards, which formed beautiful backdrops for fine sculptures. Many of these residences, like for instance Weißenstein Castle (1711–1718) in Pommersfelden and the Würzburg Residence (1720–1753), brought the formal language of Late Baroque and Rococo to extraordinary heights.

Johann Conrad Schlaun, Erbdrostenhof, 1753–1757, Münster, Germany
The challenge of this scheme lay in the awkward shape of the plot. Schlaun overcame the obstacle by creating two curved wings on either side of a slightly curved central section which meet at an acute angle, thus creating a triangular courtyard in front of the flamboyant palace façade. Schlaun was deeply influenced by Italian architecture, from Borromini's Oratorio dei Filippini in Rome to Bernini's design for the eastern elevation of the Louvre.

THE MASTERPIECE
AUGUSTUSBURG

Augustusburg, in the North-Rhine Province of Westphalia, is one of the most well-known Late Baroque residences in Germany. In 1724, Clement Augustus I Wittelsbach, Elector and Archbishop of Cologne, commissioned the architect, Johann Conrad Schlaun to design and build a palace that would reflect the prestige of his position, while simultaneously rehabilitating the ruins of the previous medieval castle on the site. Schlaun was thus faced with the task of having to create a residence that

responded to the taste for Baroque out of the ruins of a far older building. Clement's brother, Prince-Elector Karl Albert of Bavaria, was unimpressed by Schlaun's design and in 1728 he summoned his Court Architect, the Frenchman François de Cuvilliés, to Brühl from Munich to redesign the residence in order to respond to the new Rococo style. Cuvilliés converted the palace into a compact U-shaped form; the interiors were influenced by Late Baroque Italian, French and Northern European

top, left
Johann Conrad Schlaun and François de Cuvilliés, Augustusburg Castle, 1724–1740, Brühl, Germany
Initially designed by Schlaun as a hunting lodge, the project was later assigned to the French architect to the Munich Court, François de Cuvilliés, to be revamped in the new Rococo style. The exterior façade became more elegant, whilst the interior spaces were altered and refurbished to be more frivolous.

bottom, left
Dominique Girard, view of the gardens at Augustusburg Castle, begun 1728, Brühl, Germany
The favourite residence of the Prince-Elect and Archbishop of Cologne, Clement Augustus Wittelsbach, was the castle at Brühl, after which it was named. The French architect, Dominique Girard, was commissioned to design the extensive gardens, which were inspired by the gardens at Nymphenburg, near Munich. Girard planned a system of canals that encircled the gardens, the focal point being a large water feature situated on the central axis, reminiscent of the gardens in Versailles. A series of diagonal avenues links the main parterre to the wooded area.
The carefully planned arrangement of parterres, the geometric and axial layout, the manner in which the elements interweave, the choice of greenery and the circulation paths are typical of Baroque gardens, which were designed as geometric patterns circumscribed by nature. This elaborate piece of landscape architecture symbolises the orderly nature of royal power and the subjugation of society to it.

décor, embellished with frescoes and paintings by Italian artists like Carlo Carlone, who was highly sought-after by German patrons. In 1741, Balthasar Neumann drew up plans for the Grand Staircase, which was completed in 1744. As was customary, there was a grand *cour d'honneur* in the centre of the U-shape and a large, landscaped garden on the sunny southern side of the palace. In 1728, the French landscape architect, Dominique Girard, who had trained at Versailles, embarked on the design for the great parterre. He was inspired by the grand parks he had visited, such as the gardens at the Belvedere in Vienna and the gardens at Nymphenburg in Munich with their intricate flowerbeds, interspersed with water features of various kinds. As Augustusburg Palace was used as a summer residence, the Prince spent a couple of months there each year; whilst the Court spent the

remainder of the year at the sumptuous urban residence in Bonn.

A long extended avenue links the palace to the Falkenlust hunting lodge, which is a small Rococo gem that was designed by Cuvilliés and was modelled on the lodge at Amalienburg. Interestingly, the site for the palace was chosen based on the flight path of herons; herons being one of the favourite preys of falcons. The roof terrace at the hunting lodge was used as a vantage point from which falcon hunting could be observed. Cuvilliés' design created a place that could also be used as a *maison de plaisance*, a place where the Prince could relax and enjoy his private pleasures, casting off the shackles of protocol. Peter Laporterie built the *Muschelkappelle* (Shell Pavilion), a grotto-like structure, encrusted with stones, shells and crystals, which was built in close proximity to the lodge.

above, left
Balthasar Neumann, staircase at Augustusburg Castle, 1740–1746, Brühl, Germany
The vestibule at Augustusburg Castle exemplifies the successful combination of dynamic curved forms counterbalanced by the stark verticality of the paired columns and piers.

above, right
François de Cuvilliés, dining room, Augustusburg Castle, 1728–1743, Brühl, Germany
The decoration of the interior rooms was influenced by Italian and Bavarian examples and was realised with the help of Italian specialists. The ceiling of the room was painted by Carlo Innocenzo Carlone in 1743, and depicts the apotheosis of the House of Wittelsbach.

BALTHASAR NEUMANN

Balthasar Neumann is regarded as one of the greatest German Late Baroque architects. His designs display a certain playfulness and frivolity and are characterised by imaginative, elegant and complex forms which are assembled in a sophisticated, inspired manner. Neumann's work typifies 18th century 'frivolous gaiety'. Even his designs for churches are light-hearted and opulent. The young architect was fortunate enough to be introduced to members of the House of Schönborn in Franconia, which led to the commissions and building of flamboyant Late Baroque buildings, such as the Würzburg Residence and the urban restructuring of the city. Subsequent to Neumann's study trip to Paris, Vienna and Milan in around 1718, he was commissioned to design the residence at Würzburg. Neumann collaborated with numerous architects who were already famous in their own right; such as Cotte and Boffrand from France, who were both proponents of the new Rococo style. Neumann was particularly famous for his elaborate staircases, such as the staircase at Bruchsal (1732) and the staircase at Brühl Palace (1741–1744). The latter part of Neumann's career was devoted to sacred architecture; his masterpiece being the Basilica of the Fourteen Holy Helpers at Vierzehnheiligen (1743–1772) in High Franconia, one of the most famous places of pilgrimage in Germany. The church at Neresheim (1750–1753), which is far simpler in design, is elliptical in form; the light, slender columns that support the large central dome are reminiscent of Gothic architecture. Furthermore, Neumann designed the Wiesentheid Parish Church (1727–1732), the Holy Trinity Basilica at Gössweinstein, (completed in 1739), St. Paulin at Trier (begun 1734), the Church of St Cecilia in Heusenstamm (1739) as well as the highly unusual double church at Dirnstein, Laurentiuskirche, (1742–1746), where Catholics and Protestants were both able to worship simultaneously, divided only by a wall. In some instances Neumann built entire streets of new buildings, like the Theatinerstrasse in Würzburg. Neumann's final work was the single-nave Wallfahrtskirche Maria Limbach (1751–1755) near Hassfurt, the façade of which shows signs of a neo-Classicism.

below, left
Balthasar Neumann, dome of the Klosterkirche, 1750–1753, Neresheim, Germany
Neumann used the church at Neresheim to test his concept regarding the interpenetration of longitudinal and centrally-planned spaces, an ideal blend of Late Baroque and Early Classicism. Once again the plan is defined by a series of transversal oval spaces surmounted by a dome, connected to a circular temple that rests on four freestanding pairs of columns. These elements are unconnected to the side spaces and contrive to make the basilica look rather like a hall.

below, right
Balthasar Neumann, view of the interior of the Basilica of the Fourteen Holy Helpers at Vierzehnheiligen, 1743–1772, Bad Staffelstein, Germany
Neumann managed to achieve a perfect synthesis of Rococo architecture, interweaving a complex system of ovals, on the floor plan as well as in the powerfully decorated vaults. The architect avoided the traditional basilica layout by dispensing with a cupola in favour of a carefully-engineered system of intersecting vaults over the intersection. The extreme verticality of the space was obtained by fusing the original biaxial plan with that of a Latin cross. The verticality was also achieved by virtue of the fact that the centres of the two layouts do not correspond exactly.

THE MASTERPIECE
THE WÜRZBURG RESIDENCE

Since the late 17th century, the town of Würzburg in Bavaria had enjoyed a lively artistic output thanks to the presence of the House of Schönborn. In 1719, the town became the seat of the Episcopal Principality. The Würzburg Residence was originally commissioned by the Prince-Bishop, Johann Philipp Franz von Schönborn. Although the services of famous architects such as Welsch, Hildebrandt and the Frenchmen, Cotte and Boffrand were sought, it was Neumann who was the principal architect of the complex. Neumann worked on the residence for many years between 1720 and 1753. He was principally interested in creating a palatial building, concentrating on the overall shape of the exterior as well as the detail of the interior layout in order to achieve compactness and harmonious proportions. The palace is built according to a U-shaped plan with the *cour d'honneur* at the centre. Each of the two broad wings encloses another two

internal courtyards. The parapet is embellished with balusters, vases and sculptures. Despite the grandeur and scale of the palace, Neumann succeeded in his goal of creating a structured and well-balanced building.

With the exception of the large formal salons, the internal layout is arranged over two horizontal levels, with a series of interconnected rooms leading off extremely long corridors. The singularity of the residence lies in the design of the internal features such as the Grand Staircase, the octagonal *Kaisersaal* (Emperor's Hall) and the *Gartensaal* (Garden Hall) with its constricted, low ceiling. These are extraordinary spaces, where architecture, sculptural decoration and illusionistic paintings blend to form an organic work of art. The harmony and majesty of the Würzburg Residence are metaphoric for the power and prestige that the Roman Catholic Church enjoyed in Southern Germany.

Balthasar Neumann, façade of the Würzburg Residence, 1720–1753, Würzburg, Germany
The two bands of apertures with their classical pediments, the elegant string-course and projecting cornice purvey a structured, orderly appearance to the strictly symmetrical façade. The curved, projecting central body is emphasised by columns and triple-arched windows.

ST PETERSBURG: THE INVENTION OF A CAPITAL

The city of St Petersburg was founded by Peter the Great (1672–1725) during the early 18th century. In 1703, the Tsar decided to build a city named after his patron saint, St Peter, in commemoration of his victories over the Swedish and Polish armies. The new city, built along the River Neva, became the capital of the Empire in 1713. The city was built on what had formerly been a vast marshy tract of land; it flourished thanks to its strategic position by the coast, which helped to boost trade with Northern European countries. The Tsar summoned leading European architects, painters and decorators – French and Italian in particular – to build St Petersburg. This demonstrated the Tsar's eagerness to embrace Western European culture. The Italian architect, Domenico Trezzini, oversaw the first phase of the construction of the St Peter and Paul Fortress on a small island on the River Neva. The works slowed down after the death of the Tsar, but were resumed under his daughter, Tsarina Elizabeth I (1709–1762), who entrusted another Italian architect, Bartolomeo Francesco Rastrelli, with completing her father's building project. Rastrelli worked on the Winter Palace and the Imperial Residence (begun by Trezzini), until its completion in 1762. The palace, imposing in both shape and scale, was planned according to Late Baroque canons, its extended riverside façade enlivened by the skilled employment of double orders of columns and variations in the windows and tympanums. The roof parapets were adorned and animated by a large number of bronze statues. Subsequently Rastrelli went on to build the splendid Anickov and Stroganov Palaces.

Domenico Trezzini, Cathedral of St Peter and St Paul, 1714–1733, St Petersburg
The Cathedral is built in reduced Baroque style with an elegant façade crowned by a 120-metre-high German-influenced spire, which still soars up over the cityscape today. The church was one of the first stone buildings along the Neva in Peter the Great's new capital.

St Peter and Paul Fortress, 1703, St Petersburg
The fortress was built for the Tsar on an island on the Neva in order to safeguard the road to the Baltic. It was later to be transformed into one of the most imposing fortifications in Europe by the architect, Domenico Trezzini. The brick bastions, inspired by similar Dutch and Swedish buildings, surround a citadel: deemed the easiest and least costly way of protecting the city.

THE MASTERPIECE
THE PETERHOF PALACE

The Imperial Peterhof Palace lies on the Gulf of Finlandia, approximately twenty kilometres southwest of St Petersburg. As its name implies, the palace was initiated by Peter the Great who commissioned it to be built in 1714 as his country residence. The Tsar had become acquainted with the latest trends in art and architecture during a lengthy trip to Europe; he was fascinated by architecture and followed the building of his new residence closely.

The Tsar dreamed of creating a royal palace to rival Versailles, thus he summoned the French architect, Alexandre Le Blond (1679–1719), who was also a renowned garden designer, to take charge of the project. The palace and landscaped gardens were eventually inaugurated in 1723; waterfalls, fed by a canal downstream of the North Sea, adorned the park. Extensions were continued in Late Baroque style; this included the Hermitage (1721–1725), which was a pavilion used by the Tsar for private dinners. Peterhof became the Imperial family's official summer residence; during the winter months they sojourned at the so-called 'Winter Palace' in St Petersburg.

Façade overlooking the Marly-le-Roy fountain, 1714–1751, Peterhof, St Petersburg
Nicola Michetti designed a large water feature and fountain modelled on the fountain at Marly-le-Roy at Versailles, from which it took its name. The design illustrates Michetti's familiarity with Northern European landscape architecture. The great waterfall is adorned with seventeen statues, twenty-nine bas-reliefs, one-hundred-and-forty-two water jets and sixty-four waterspouts. The groups of statues allude allegorically to the Russian victory over Charles XII of Sweden during the dispute for the outlet in the Baltic Sea.

BARTOLOMEO FRANCESCO RASTRELLI

Bartolomeo Francesco Rastrelli (1700–1771) was the most famous Russian Late Baroque architect, his style was also known as 'St Petersburg Baroque' or 'Rastrelli style'. Rastrelli was of Italian origin and had travelled to Russia from France with his father, a sculptor, at the age of fifteen. His earliest work was carried out during the 1730s, but it was during the following twenty years until the 1750s that his prolific output demonstrated the true extent of his skill and technical proficiency. Rastrelli was the first Court Architect of Elizabeth I; it was his finesse that transformed St Petersburg and the surrounding area into a magnificent celebratory urban arena. As well as extending the Peterhof Imperial Palace from 1745 onwards, Rastrelli also built the sumptuous Voroncov and Stroganov Palaces (1750–1754) in the city and oversaw the restructuring and extension of the Catherine Palace (now Tsarskoe Selo, 1752–1756); an excellent example of Rococo architecture. The architect also designed and built the Summer Palace (1740–1744, now destroyed), the Smol'nyi Monastery (1748–1755) and embarked on the imposing Winter Palace in 1755. Despite the fact that a great many of his Rococo interiors no longer exist through subsequent alterations or wars, the exteriors of his palaces, decorated with golden and coloured friezes and cornices, elegant columns and luminous windows nevertheless demonstrate his mastery of 17th century French and Italian courtly Baroque. Rastrelli was not only a gifted imitator of established styles; his brilliance lay in his ability to interpret and reformulate certain elements in order to create an architectural style particular to St Petersburg and the surrounding region. Rastrelli's architecture achieved a harmonious blend of a myriad of styles: Baroque and Rococo, Renaissance and Mannerist, traditional Russian and Western. Despite their opulence, Rastrelli's palaces contrived to look composed and orderly and were never excessively flamboyant. He restricted the height of his buildings to three storeys which was to remain the general rule for building heights in St Petersburg; providing a sense of order, elegance and harmony that still characterises the city today. It was only the rise of the Neo-Classicism that eventually put a halt to 'St Petersburg' Baroque at Court. Rastrelli spent his remaining years searching, in vain, for a new patron.

Bartolomeo Francesco Rastrelli, Winter Palace, façade overlooking the River Neva, 1754–1762, St Petersburg
The articulation of the exterior façades of the enormous block with its internal courtyard is clearly inspired by the Strogonov Palace (1750–1754), where Rastrelli had managed to find his own signature style. The elevation facing the River Neva is adorned with colossal columns, while the remaining façades have alternating plastic projections and more neutral elements. The rather sober double-order façades are richly decorated with stuccoes, from the various window frames to the numerous statues on the roof parapet and the pediment on the projecting gable. A wide colour-palette serves to emphasise the rhythmic sequence of the individual elements that creates a well modulated ensemble: lime green wall planes, white columns and cornices, lemon yellow capitals and black sculptures.

THE MASTERPIECE
CATHERINE PALACE

The Imperial summer residence – formerly known as Catherine Palace, now known as Tsarskoe Selo – lies twenty-four kilometres south of St Petersburg. Tsar Peter the Great (1672–1725) had subdivided the land around the capital and given it to members of his family and other members of the aristocracy, so that the city and surrounding area could be developed with new roads, palaces and gardens. Tsarskoe Selo Palace is an important example of 18th century Russian architecture; its alterations testify to the continued evolution of taste, also where interior decoration was concerned. The various architects who worked on the palace left their personal indelible imprints on the complex, culminating in a residence that displayed both Rococo and Classical characteristics. In 1717, Catherine I summoned the German architect, Johann Friedrich Braunstein, to reconstruct the former timber structure in stone and extend it to be double-storey. The private sphere was situated on the ground floor whilst the reception rooms were situated on the upper floor. The Italian architect, Domenico Trezzini, was requested to design the rooms in a Dutch style, an aesthetic

which was admired for its noble sobriety. In 1741, Elizabeth I decided to extend and furnish the palace in the latest style in vogue, placing one of the most renowned Russian architects, Mikhail Zemtsov, in charge of the entire project. However, it was one of his pupils, Andrei Kvasov, who began the renovation in 1744. Kvasov created two narrow, double-storey galleries that were linked to two stone buildings, one of which contained a small chapel and the other, the grand reception room and conservatory. The project was continued by Giuseppe Trezzini and then later by Seva Tchevakinskij, who created gardens above both galleries, inspired by the Hanging Gardens of Babylon. Bartolomeo Francesco Rastrelli took over the entire project in 1749, but was asked shortly after its completion, in 1751, to carry out further alterations for his dissatisfied client. Rastrelli heightened the galleries, thereby creating a uniformly triple-storey building and a single, harmonious front for the façade, as was later employed at the Winter Palace. Thus Catherine I's formally (relatively-speaking) modest home was transformed into an elegant and regal palace.

above, left
Catherine Palace, begun 1717, Tsarskoe Selo, Russia
On the occasion of the consecration of the Palace church on the 30th July 1756, the palace was adorned with massive gilded decoration both on the interior and the exterior. Over 100 kilograms of gold-leaf were needed to make the stunning decorations, including all the friezes, capitals and sculptures (caryatids, globes). However, given the harsh Russian climate, the sparkling golden gilding did not prove to be very durable and was eventually repainted in dark ochre.

above, right
Amber Room, Catherine Palace, begun 1717, Tsarkoe Selo, Russia
The Amber Room was created in the Berlin Castle (now destroyed) in 1701, and consisted of a space entirely lined with amber panels, described by enthralled eyewitnesses at the time as being "the eighth wonder of the world."

ENGLAND

The evolution of Baroque art in England was circumscribed by unfavourable circumstances, namely: hostility to Catholicism and Papism, a refusal to recognise
absolute princely power, the national tradition of 'Euro-scepticism' and finally, loyalty to their medieval heritage. England could not countenance the rhetorical
Counter Reformation style, nor the dramatic perspectives and unlimited axes of
Royal French architecture. During the years spanning between the reigns of Queen
Anne and George I, the aristocracy became even more closely-knit and inward-
looking; architecture correspondingly went through a specifically English Late
Baroque phase. English Baroque was vaguely accepted between the late 17th century and the 1730s, while the preferred architectural style continued to be Classical. Nicholas Hawksmoor (1671–1736) collaborated with John Vanbrugh
(1664–1726) on the two most overtly Baroque country houses on the British Isles:
Castle Howard (1699-1712) in Yorkshire – the interiors are adorned with frescoes
by Giovanni Antonio Pellegrini – and Blenheim Palace (1705–1724) in Oxfordshire.
These two monumental residences by Vanbrugh are testament to the architects'
talent for assembling volumes in a meaningful way without neglecting even the
smallest detail, thus characterising every single element in a refined and eclectic
way. Both residences echo Christopher Wren's grandiose style, yet on an even
more monumental scale. Despite being inspired by a variety of precursors, the
various elements of both buildings achieve a harmonious synthesis, for instance,
the Gothic castle at Versailles, Palladian villas, as well as Austrian and German
palace layouts.

**John Vanbrugh and Nicholas Hawksmoor,
view of Blenheim Palace, 1705–1724,
Woodstock, England**
Blenheim Palace is a rare testament to
the integration of Baroque canons into
English architecture. The enormous
palace was a gift from the Queen to the
Duke of Marlborough after his victory
over Louis XIV at the Battle of Blenheim in 1704. The project was started
by John Vanbrugh but completed by
Nicholas Hawksmoor. As in Castle
Howard, a large atrium and a central
reception room are situated on the longitudinal axis, whilst the kitchens, stables and stores are situated along the
transversal axis. The castle displays
some typically English architectural
elements, like the Corinthian portico,
which is reminiscent of Inigo Jones's
designs for Whitehall and Wren's
designs for Greenwich Hospital, whilst
the chimney-like corner towers are
reminiscent of Elizabethan castles.

PORTUGAL

The history of Portuguese architecture differs considerably from that of its neigh-bour, Spain. During the early 18th century, under King John V (1706–1750), Rome was the benchmark for Portuguese architecture and their desperate efforts to build a second Rome on the banks of the Tago River.

The King's emissaries had procured models of all the most important Roman monuments and learnt about Papal ceremony and protocol. The discovery of gold and diamond reserves in the mines of Portugal's colony, Brazil, enabled the coun-try to launch into an extraordinary push for transformation, to become one of the wealthiest powers in the world. One notorious example of the endless self-publi-cising ambitions of the sovereign – which was also to drag the country into bank-ruptcy – was the project for the Mafra Monastery: a colossal scheme, developed by the German architect, Johann Friedrich Ludwig. Construction on the Palace/Monastery at Mafra began in 1717. The project was a vainglorious attempt to rival the Escorial in Spain, a building that had echoes of St Peter's, St Ignatius and Palazzo Montecitorio, with the accent on civil rather than religion architecture. Two fatal events were to lead to an abrupt change in building policy: firstly the death of King John V in 1750 and secondly the disastrous earthquake of 1755, which razed nearly two thirds of the city of Lisbon to the ground. The reconstruc-tion efforts led to a complete rebuilding programme, involving grand-scale archi-tectural projects that could well be regarded as forerunners for 19th century urban planning.

Bom Jesus do Monte, 1784–1811, Braga, Portugal
Bom Jesus is a sanctuary built on the crest of a hill; the layered steps up to the church display a curious blend of Christian, Antique and pagan motifs.

Mateus Vicente de Oliveira, Royal Palace, begun 1747, Queluz, Portugal
The Portuguese architect, Mateus Vicente de Oliveira, created this ele-gant building around a large *cour d'honneur*. The French-style interior furnishings include a wealth of rocaille decoration. The gardens, designed by Jean-Baptiste Robillon, landscaped in 1758, were inspired by Le Nôtre and are redolent of the sophisticated taste of the *Ancien Régime*.

SPAIN

The rise of the Counter Reformation and the rigorous centralisation of power were catalysts in the development of Spanish architecture during the 18th century. Architecture during that era was characterised by the increasing disregard of Classical harmony in favour of a more emphatic hierarchy of individual elements, through the plastic treatment of walls, the use of different and contrasting materials and an over-abundance of exterior decoration.

The sacristy of La Cartuja in Granada, for example, displays formal Classical elements which have been swathed in decoration and liberally reinterpreted in stucco-work.

Francisco Hurtado Izquierdo's highly original decorative forms, drawn from Classical elements which were then fragmented and multiplied kaleidoscopically, earned him a place in the vanguard of Spanish architecture. A new local tradition, known as 'Churrigueresque' (named after the Churriguera family from Catalan) emerged within a short space of time. This movement displayed an exaggerated version of Baroque, characterised by highly flamboyant and exuberant sculptural ornamentation.

Churriguesque architecture was noteworthy for its extreme floral decoration, created in such profusion and with such a variety of plastic forms that it took on a unique value of its own, creating spectacular effects and utterly masking the structure of buildings. Spanish heterogeneity subsequently gave way to courtly Bourbon art, largely inspired by Italian and French Classicism. This trend was initially led by a group of Italian architects such as Giovan Battista Sacchetti and Filippo Juvarra – authors of the Royal Palace in Madrid.

below, left
José Benito Churriguera, façade of the Cathedral of Santiago de Compostela, 1738–1749, Spain
The façade of one of the most famous European places of pilgrimage displays a harmonious mélange of all Late Baroque elements and epitomises the flamboyance and exterior articulation of Spanish Baroque.
The monumentality and Classical shapes contrast with the high relief of the surfaces that are swathed in ornamentation. The Romanesque portal – flanked on either side by towers – is almost completely hidden behind the façade, with its Baroque stairway that links the street level to the entry level above.

below, right
Francisco de Hurtado Izquierdo, Sacristy of La Cartuja, 1732–1745, Granada, Spain
In the past, critics were known to attribute the quintessential decadence of Spanish art to over-elaborate, over-exaggerated decoration; the constricted Sacristy at the Cartuja Monastery in Granada is an apt example of this excess. Despite the overwhelming encrustation of the stucco-work, the structure of the building remains clearly visible. The various decorative motifs inspired by Classical elements, such as capitals, cornices, volutes, chandeliers and the so-called 'pig's ears', all serve to mask the buttressing of the wall structure, creating a surreal play of light and decoration. The rhetorical Baroque language became a dialogue between fleeting, ephemeral elements, in a similar manner to the aesthetic of Rococo that was developing at the same time.

THE MASTERPIECE
THE *TRANSPARENTE* ALTARPIECE

An unusual devotional feature of large Spanish churches, the '*sacrarium*' was also one of the original features of Spanish religious architecture. Sacrariums were used for the preservation and worship of the Holy Sacrament and were frequently kept in large tabernacles, the '*Transparente*' (translated as 'transparent'), which sometimes extended almost as high as the ceilings. The most astonishing and complex example of these *Transparente* is Narciso Tomé's *Transparente* in Toledo Cathedral. Narciso Tomé (1690–1742), originated from a Spanish family of skilled sculptors and carvers, and was appointed Cathedral Architect in 1721. Tomé built an incredible work of art in the centre of the building, thus enabling the *sacrarium*, (previously poorly lit) to become dazzlingly visible.

The sculptor installed an extraordinary, unrivalled architectural device directly behind the high altar: a carved marble, jasper, stucco and bronze wall in lavish Late Baroque style, which took over a decade to complete. This particular plastic, architectural structure consists of a kind of concave double-storey retable which includes a sculptural ensemble of the Virgin and Child on the lower section and a depiction of the Last Supper on the upper section above. The retable ties in symbolically with the tabernacle containing the Holy Sacrament. The *sacrarium* was positioned so that the choir as well as the congregation and pilgrims in the nave would be able to see it simultaneously. An opening was cut in the ceiling above it, forming an oculus to allow a shaft of natural light to illuminate the entire tabernacle.

Floating clouds and golden rays symbolise the Eucharistic sun, flying angels and animated Biblical figures illuminated by shafts of daylight to create a magnificent theatrical effect, almost as if the altar were enveloped in supernatural light, engendering feelings of godliness in those beholding it. A Latin inscription on the bottom right-hand corner bears the author's signature.

Narciso Tomé, view of the *Transparente*, 1721–1732, Toledo Cathedral, Spain
Narciso Tomé's *Transparente* is possibly the most spectacular and theatrical piece of Spanish Late Baroque architecture; in itself an incredible work of art. It transformed the traditional Holy Sacrament tabernacle into a plastic/architectural structure where architecture and sculpture, stuccoes and gilded bronzes, illuminated from on high, create a masterful blend of theatre and flamboyance.

LATIN AMERICA

The European architecture imported into Latin America had a decidedly Spanish and Portuguese flavour, as would be expected as their colonisers came from the Iberian Peninsula. The new imported vocabularies took a while to take root in the indigenous populations in Latin America; but in time their original and exuberant interpretation of European Baroque blossomed and continued to flourish for a couple of centuries. Spain and Portugal were exposed to different cultures and artistic traditions; Islamic and Catholic for example, intermingled with the Mudejar and Plateresque style. Equally, Latin America had its own unique combination of different vocabularies, ranging from Late Gothic to Renaissance and Baroque. From the 16th century, when the mendicant orders built their mission churches, the mélange of styles was a dominant feature of many churches and monasteries in Mexico. There was an obvious disparity and time lag between the style of the colonial motherland and the style adopted in the colonised territories. This was certainly the case in the development of 'Hispano-American' Baroque that was characterised by boisterous decorative detail, vitality and a real *horror vacui*, (Latin for 'fear of empty space'). Hispano-American Baroque did not employ the typical Baroque spatial compositions, but rather relied on opulent and lavish decoration, with the repetition of certain stylistic features. Façades became works of art in their own right, extremely complex and difficult to decipher. They resembled great open-air retablos (beautifully carved wooden Spanish-type altars) with a powerful presence of *éstipites* – non load-bearing posts shaped like elongated upside-down pyramids.

below, left
Santo Domingo, San Cristóbal de las Casas, c. 1700, Mexico
Mexican churches were frequently variations on the architectural tenants of Spanish Baroque. Façades were transformed into displays of rich figurative and ornamental repertoires, structurally similar to retables.

below, right
The Merced Monastery Church, c. 1767, Antigua, Antigua and Barbuda
Merced Monastery was one of the most important monasteries on Antigua. Bold volumes and use of colours create a lively and dynamic harmony. The façade displays a combination of lavish ornamentation and animated reliefs depicting God's bounty, with Classical themes interpreted in an entirely Baroque rhetoric.

left
Aleijadinho, Church of San Francesco d'Assisi, 1765–1775, Ouro Preto, Brazil
Arcuate plans, centralised internal spaces and curved façades behind which the bell-towers are tucked, are some of the most original characteristics of Brazilian architecture that are displayed in this eccentric church in Ouro Preto. Aleijadinho is one of the very few documented Latin American architects, although very little is known about him.

below
Façade of Torre Tagle Palace, 1735, Lima, Chile
During the 18th century, Peruvian architecture was inspired by European prototypes; the buildings produced there were more elegant and refined than those conceived in Mexico. The façade of Torre Tagle Palace was inspired by Andalusian palatial façades, its harmony and elegance commensurate with its status as capital of the Viceroy.

Unlike Europe, the colonies revelled in and exalted architecture, creating wonderfully decorative schemes, while leaving the structures fairly simple and rectilinear. Clearly the climate was different, as were the available materials, there was also a cross-pollination of different local building techniques and decorative schemes unfamiliar back in Europe (for instance, tropical flowers and exotic fruit).

In South America architecture developed along different lines; in Peru, for example, two separate regional styles developed: one in the Andes mountains and the other along the coast and on the plains. Even the building techniques and materials differed in these two geographic areas: stone in the mountains and sun-dried clay bricks and compacted earth along coastal areas. The vaults and ceilings of buildings in Peru were constructed with reeds mixed with chalk and supported by a wooden or brick (*quincha*) frame, the structure was light, low-cost and especially suited to unstable seismic areas.

South America adhered more closely to the architecture of its colonisers than Mexico with less elaborate façades, more similar to their Italian and Spanish origins. Naturally, there was a delay in the evolution of styles in these colonies, with an obvious eclectic mix of vocabularies (Gothic, Italian, Mudejar etc.), and an ability to employ them with harmony and panache.

INDEX OF PLACES

PHOTOGRAPHIC CREDITS

© 2012 Prestel Publishers, Munich · London · New York, for the English edition
© 2012 Mondadori Electa SpA , Milan, for the original edition, all rights reserved

Prestel Publishers, Munich
A member of Verlagsgruppe Random House GmbH

Prestel Verlag
Neumarkter Straße 28
81673 Munich
Tel. +49 (0)89 4136-0
Fax +49 (0)89 4136-2335

Prestel Publishing Ltd.
4 Bloomsbury Place
London WC1A 2QA
Tel. +44 (0)20 7323-5004
Fax +44 (0)20 7636-8004

Prestel Publishing
900 Broadway, Suite 603
New York, NY 10003
Tel. +1 (212) 995-2720
Fax +1 (212) 995-2733

www.prestel.com

Library of Congress Control Number is available;
British Library Cataloguing-in-Publication Data:
a catalogue record for this book is available from the
British Library; Deutsche Nationalbibliothek holds
a record of this publication in the Deutsche National-
bibliografie; detailed bibliographical data can be
found under: http://dnb.d-nb.de

Prestel books are available worldwide. Please
contact your nearest bookseller or one of the
above addresses for information concerning
your local distributor.

Editorial direction: Stella Sämann
Translation: Bridget Mason
Copyediting: Anna Roos, Bern
Cover: Sofarobotnik, Augsburg & Munich
Production: Astrid Wedemeyer
Typesetting: Wolfram Söll, Munich
Printing and Binding: Mondadori Printing, Verona

Printed in Italy

ISBN 978-3-7913-4595-6

Random House Publishers FSC-DEU-0100
The FSC-certified paper Respecta Satin has been
supplied by Burgo cartiere (Italy).